CLAIM YOUR REFUND

TODAY AND ENJOY YOUR SAVINGS

By

SHAHINUL KHALISDAR

DEDICATION

This book is dedicated to my beloved wife, Muna Al-Neaimi, whose unwavering love and support have been my foundation through every challenge and triumph. To my father, whose wisdom and encouragement continue to inspire my journey, and to all those who believe in the power of perseverance and lifelong learning. Your faith in me has made this endeavor possible, and I am forever grateful.

ACKNOWLEDGEMETS

I would like to express my deepest gratitude to my wife, Muna Al-Neaimi, who supported me throughout the journey of writing this book. To my father, who taught me to write, your encouragement and belief in me made all the difference. I am also grateful to the editor and project manager who provided invaluable feedback and inspiration along the way. This accomplishment would not have been possible without your unwavering support and guidance.

Clean Energy Credits after 2025

The federal energy tax credit landscape will change significantly due to the OBBBA, which was signed into law on July 4, 2025. This legislation has either repealed or modified various clean energy tax credits. Below is a summary of the affected credits and their eligibility termination dates:

- **Clean Vehicle Credit (IRC Section §30D)**
  Eligibility ends for vehicles acquired after September 30, 2025.

- **Used Clean Vehicle Credit (IRC Section §25E)**
  Eligibility ends for vehicles acquired after September 30, 2025.

- **Alternative Fuel Refueling Property Credit (IRC Section §30C)**
  Eligibility ends for property placed in service after June 30, 2026.

- **Residential Clean Energy Credit (IRC Section §25D)**
  Eligibility ends for expenditures made after December 31, 2025.

- **Energy Efficient Home Improvement Credit (IRC Section §25C)**
  Eligibility ends for property placed in service after December 31, 2025.

These changes mark a significant shift in the federal approach to clean energy incentives starting in 2025.

ABOUT THE AUTHOR

The author is a passionate tax advisor dedicated to sharing fundamental tax knowledge and helping taxpayers file their returns accurately. With a background shaped by personal experiences and a commitment to continuous learning, the author strives to connect with readers on a meaningful level. This book represents the culmination of years of work as a tax professional, curiosity, and the unwavering support of loved ones. The author holds a Master's degree from William Howard Taft University (WHTU) School of Government and Law, Master of Science in Taxation (MST) and is an IRS-licensed tax practitioner known as an Enrolled Agent.

Table of Contents

INTRODUCTION

"Unlock the secrets of the 1040 form to gain a better understanding to effectively do your Tax Return"

This is a comprehensive guide to Form 1040 and the various forms included with it for filing your tax return. The normal filing deadline is April 15, and if April 15 falls on a weekend or holiday, the deadline is usually extended to the next business day, which is typically Monday.

As a tax professional for 25 years, I'm often asked: "What is Form 1040 and why does it matter?" If you're unsure about needing it or qualifying, you're not the only one. Let's break it down together and explore who can benefit from this essential book, whether you're a small business owner or an individual looking to file your taxes with ease.

I intend to author a book on Form 1040 with the aim of providing a comprehensive foundation for taxpayers to understand its key components and primary considerations. Of course, the Tax Law changes when a new USA Administration assumes its political authority every four years. This book serves as the complete guide to Form 1040 for individuals and small businesses, offering solutions to all essential tax questions and forms.

A guide to Form 1040.

What Is Income Tax?

Income tax is a required payment the government levies on a person's or organization's earnings, whether from wages or from sources such as business, interest, and dividends. This revenue is a major source of funding for public services, and the government needs to pay employees and maintain infrastructure.

The Evolution of Income Tax in the U.S.

In 1862, the U.S. took a major step by introducing its first income tax to support the Civil War effort. Although this initial tax was repealed once the war ended, it was reinstated with the Revenue Act of 1913, leading the IRS to release Form 1040 that same year. Today, all required tax return filers use Form 1040. It is important to understand that the U.S. follows a progressive tax system in which higher earners pay at higher tax rates.

The Basics

Often referred to as the individual income tax, this levy applies to wages, salaries, and other forms of individual income. It is important to note that this tax is primarily levied at the federal level. Additionally, 41 states and the District of Columbia impose a comprehensive individual income tax on wages and salaries; however, these state-level taxes are assessed only on taxable income rather than on all sources of income. Deductions, exemptions, and credits in the income tax system often lower the actual taxes owed, so individuals rarely pay taxes on their entire income.

Personal Tax Credits and Deductions

This book discusses the key personal credits available for the Tax Return, outlining the eligibility requirements, benefit amounts, and the process for claiming them. It is specifically designed for tax professionals preparing returns for individual taxpayers, including those with dependents, who seek to maximize available tax benefits.

The IRS offers two types of deductions: standard deduction and the itemized deduction. An adjustment to income is a different type of deduction for certain personal expenses, along with various credits that reduce your taxable income. A deduction reduces the amount of income subject to tax, while a credit reduces the actual tax bill.

For example, if you earn $90,000 but qualify for $20,000 in deductions, your taxable income effectively drops to $70,000.

On the other hand, tax credits are a legally qualified way to reduce what you owe directly. They usually help middle- to lower-income families. For example, if your tax bill is $10,000 and you qualify for $4,500 in credits, you'll only have to pay $5,500 only.

Tax credits fall into several categories, with the primary distinction between refundable and nonrefundable credits.

Refundable Credits

Refundable tax credits can result in a refund even if you have no tax liability. If the credit exceeds your tax liability, the IRS will issue a refund for the difference. Notable examples of refundable credits include:

- Earned Income Tax Credit (EITC)
- Additional Child Tax Credit

The Child Tax Credit (CTC) provides significant tax benefits for families with children. For the tax year 2025, the credit is partially refundable, meaning eligible taxpayers can receive a portion of the credit as a refund even if they do not owe any income tax. The CTC is valued at up to $2,200, with adjustments for inflation expected in future years.

It's important to understand that while the CTC can reduce your tax liability to zero, a portion of it is refundable for 2025. This refundable portion is known as the Additional Child Tax Credit (ACTC). For 2025, taxpayers may receive up to $1,700 per qualifying child as a refund. However, any remaining amount beyond the tax owed will not be refunded.

Nonrefundable Credits

In contrast, nonrefundable tax credits can reduce your tax liability to zero; they do not result in a refund or provide money back if you do not owe any taxes. You can benefit from these credits only to the extent of your tax obligation. Examples of nonrefundable credits include:

- Child and Dependent Care Credit
- Retirement Savings Contributions Credit (Saver's Credit)
- Lifetime Learning Credit (LLC)

Partially Refundable Credits

There is also a category of credits that combines refundable and nonrefundable features. These partially refundable credits can reduce your tax liability to zero, but any excess may be refundable. A prime example of this hybrid structure is the American Opportunity Tax Credit (AOTC), which has both refundable and nonrefundable components.

"Understanding these classifications can help taxpayers maximize their benefits when filing their tax returns."

An Important Reminder

Keep in mind that your taxable income is determined by subtracting either your itemized or standard deductions from your adjusted gross income (AGI). Having a clear grasp of this process can help you make the most of your tax planning.

The standard deduction is a predetermined dollar amount that lowers your taxable income, serving as an alternative to itemizing specific expenses. This amount is adjusted each year for inflation and differs based on your tax filing status, age, and whether you are blind. Approximately 90% of taxpayers opt for the standard deduction due to its simplicity and the likelihood of resulting in a lower tax bill compared to itemizing deductions.

The standard deduction amount varies annually, influenced by inflation adjustments and depending on your filing status, which can be one of five categories: Single, Married Filing Jointly or Qualifying Surviving Spouse, Head of Household, and Married Filing Separately. Being aware of the standard deduction amount each year is essential, as it changes and directly impacts your taxable income.

Special Circumstances:

Age and Blindness: If you or your spouse are 65 or older and/or blind by the end of the tax year, you are typically eligible for an additional standard deduction. For the 2025 tax year, this extra amount is $2,000 for single or head of household filers and $1,600 per qualifying person for married taxpayers.

Dependents: If you can be claimed as a dependent by another taxpayer, your standard deduction for 2025 is limited to the higher of (1) $1,350 or (2) your earned income plus $450, but not exceeding the basic standard deduction amount for your filing status.

New Senior Deduction: For tax years 2025 through 2028, individuals aged 65 and older may qualify for a separate new additional deduction of up to $6,000 (per qualifying person) provided their modified adjusted gross income (MAGI) is below specific thresholds. This deduction is available even for those who choose to itemize.

Standard vs. Itemized Deductions:

Taxpayers must decide between taking the standard deduction or itemizing their deductions on Schedule A (Form 1040). It is advisable to select the option that leads to a lower tax liability.

- **Standard Deduction:**
  A fixed and straightforward amount that eliminates the need to document individual expenses.
- **Itemized Deductions:**
  A cumulative total of precise, eligible expenses, which may encompass mortgage interest, state and local taxes (subject to limits), and charitable contributions.

No Tax on Tips Deduction

- **Eligibility Requirements:**
  You must have a valid Social Security number for work in the U.S.
  Your tips must be reported on either Form W-2, Form 1099, or another specified statement provided to you, or reported directly by you on Form 4137.

- **Deduction Transition:**
  Tax Year 2025 is a transition year; reasonable documentation will suffice for the deduction.
  In Tax Year 2026, employers will report this information on Form W-2.

- **Reporting Tips:**
  Tipped workers must report their monthly tip totals to their employer using Form 4070A or a similar form. It's advisable to keep a daily log for accuracy.
  Qualified tips include voluntary cash or charged tips received from customers or through tip sharing, provided they are properly documented and reported.

- **Deduction Limits:**
  The maximum deduction for tips received is $25,000 per tax return.

For self-employed individuals, the deductible amount cannot exceed their net income from the specific trade or business in which the tips were earned.

Self-employed individuals in a specified service trade or business (SSTB) under Section 199A are not eligible, nor are employees whose employers are in an SSTB. Additionally, taxpayers filing as married filing separately are not eligible.

- **Taxpayer Considerations:**

The deduction is available to both itemizing and non-itemizing taxpayers.

The "No Tax on Tips" deduction is classified as a below-the-line deduction, meaning it does not reduce adjusted gross income (AGI) and does not affect Earned Income Tax Credit (EITC) calculations.

It's important to note that the "No Tax on Tips" deduction does not eliminate Social Security or Medicare tax withholdings on tip income, so your paycheck will not reflect a change in withholding amounts.

Income Tax Impact

The new tips deduction reduces federal taxable income, but tips are still subject to Social Security and Medicare (FICA) taxes. Despite the name, the provision allows for a deduction from federal income tax rather than a total tax exclusion.

Filing the Deduction

You can claim the tip deduction directly on your tax return, even without itemizing.

Example: If you are a hairstylist who reports $25,000 in tips in 2025:

- For income tax, you can deduct $25,000 from your federal taxable income under the new tips deduction.
- For FICA taxes, you will still pay Social Security and Medicare taxes on the full $25,000 of tips.
- On your tax return, you do not need to itemize; simply claim the deduction directly on your Schedule 1-A (Form 1040), Part II.

Filing Status Considerations

The federal tip deduction is not available to all filing statuses. Specifically, taxpayers who are married filing separately cannot claim this deduction. The tip deduction, introduced by the "One Big Beautiful Bill" for tax years 2025 through 2028, has several eligibility requirements and limitations beyond just filing status:

- **Filing Status:**
  Married individuals must file a joint return to be eligible for the deduction. The deduction is available for single filers but not for those using the "married filing separately" status.
- **Income Limits:**
  The deduction begins to phase out for taxpayers with a modified adjusted gross income (MAGI) over $150,000 for single filers and $300,000 for those married filing jointly.

- **Occupation Type:**
  Tips must come from an occupation that "customarily and regularly receives tips" before 2025, as determined by the Treasury Department. Certain specified service trades or businesses (SSTBs), such as those in health, law, or accounting, are ineligible.
- **Reporting:**
  Qualified tips must be reported to the IRS, either by an employer on Form W-2 or 1099, or directly by the taxpayer on Form 4137.

Social Security Number:

"A valid Social Security Number is required to claim the deduction. "

Reporting Requirements

Employers and other payers must file information returns with the IRS (or Social Security Administration) and provide statements to taxpayers detailing certain cash tips received and the occupation of the tip recipient.

No Tax on Overtime Deduction

You must have a social security number valid for work in the U.S. Income eligible for the deduction is capped at $12,500 for singles and $25,000 for married filing jointly.

Those with higher modified adjusted gross income (MAGI) may only be able to claim a partial deduction as the benefit begins to phase out, starting at $150,000 for singles and $300,000 for married filing jointly.

The deduction is not available for people using the married filing separately status.

The new overtime pay deduction reduces federal taxable income, but overtime pay remains subject to Social Security and Medicare (FICA) taxes. No Tax on Overtime is a below-the-line deduction, meaning it doesn't reduce adjusted gross income. It does not impact Earned Income Tax Credit (EITC) calculations.

Understanding the Overtime Deduction and Its Phase-Out

The overtime deduction is a beneficial tax break for workers who earn additional income through overtime hours. However, this deduction is subject to limitations, particularly impacting higher earners as their income increases.

Phase-Out Thresholds

- **Income Threshold:**
  The overtime deduction starts to phase out for individuals with a modified adjusted gross income (MAGI) not exceeding $150,000 for single filers and $300,000 for those married filing jointly.

- **Deduction Reduction:**
  For every $1,000 earned above the specified income threshold, the deduction is reduced by $100.

Full Deductions

For example, if you are a single filer with a MAGI of $150,000 and receive $10,000 in qualified overtime pay, your MAGI is exactly at the threshold. Provided you meet all qualifications; you can deduct the full $10,000.

Partial Deductions

If your situation changes and you are a single filer with a MAGI of $200,000 and receive $12,500 in qualified overtime pay, your MAGI exceeds the threshold by $50,000. Consequently, your deduction will be reduced by $5,000, allowing you a deduction of $7,500 based on the calculation:

- Reduction: $5,000 [($50,000 ÷ $1,000) = 50 × $100].
- Final Deduction: $12,500 – $5,000 = $7,500.

No Deduction

In another scenario, if you are a single filer with a MAGI of $275,000 and you receive $10,000 in overtime pay, your MAGI surpasses the threshold by $125,000. In this case, the deduction is wholly eliminated because the reduction of $12,500 exceeds your qualified overtime pay.

Married Filing Jointly

For married couples who file jointly, if you and your spouse earn a combined income of $290,000 and receive $25,000 in qualified overtime pay, your MAGI of $290,000 is below the $300,000 threshold, allowing for a full deduction of $25,000. However, if your MAGI were to increase to $310,000, the deduction would be reduced by $1,000, resulting in a total deduction of $24,000.

- Reduction: $1,000 [$10,000 ÷ $1,000 = 10 × $100].
- Final Deduction: $25,000 – $1,000 = $24,000.

Conclusion

It's important to note that tax law changes can have varied effects based on individual circumstances. Staying informed about new provisions related to deductions, such as those discussed here, is crucial. Anticipating how these changes might influence your returns will better equip you to provide knowledgeable service and advice as the tax season approaches.

No Tax on Car Loan Interest Deduction

Under the provisions of the OBBBA, taxpayers can deduct up to $10,000 in qualified interest paid on loans for new passenger vehicles purchased between 2025 and 2028. This initiative aims to support domestic auto manufacturing and alleviate financial burdens for car buyers. For Tax Year 2025, the No Tax on Car Loan Interest deduction will be reported on Schedule 1-A (Form 1040).

Phase-Out Thresholds for the Deduction

The deduction begins to phase out based on Modified Adjusted Gross Income (MAGI):

For individuals, the phase-out starts at a MAGI over $100,000, including those filing as married filing separately. For joint filers, the threshold is $200,000.

The deduction reduces by $200 for every $1,000 earned above the threshold. As a result, single filers will not qualify for the deduction at $150,000 in MAGI, and joint filers at $250,000.

Examples of Deduction Calculation

Single Filer Example: A single filer with a MAGI of $110,000 is $10,000 over the threshold. The deduction is reduced by $200 for each $1,000 over. In this case, $10,000 excess MAGI divided by $1,000 equals 10 increments, leading to a total reduction of $2,000. Thus, the maximum available deduction would be $10,000 minus $2,000, resulting in an $8,000 deduction.

Married Filer Example: A married couple filing jointly with a MAGI of $255,000 exceeds the phase-out threshold by $55,000. This means $55,000 divided by $1,000 yields 55 increments. Multiplying by $200 results in an $11,000 reduction. Since the maximum deduction is $10,000 and the reduction surpasses this amount, they are ineligible for any deduction on car loan interest.

Eligibility for the New Deduction

From 2025 through 2028, individuals may deduct interest paid on loans used to purchase qualified vehicles, as long as:

The vehicle is intended for personal use and meets specific eligibility criteria.

Lease payments are not eligible.

The maximum deduction available is $10,000.

Qualified Interest Criteria

To qualify for the deduction, interest must meet these conditions:

- The loan must be originated after December 31, 2024.
- The vehicle must be new, with no prior use by the taxpayer (used vehicles do not qualify).
- The vehicle must be for personal use and secured by a lien on the vehicle.

If a qualifying vehicle loan is refinanced, the interest on the refinanced amount generally remains eligible for the deduction.

Definition of a Qualified Vehicle

A qualified vehicle is defined as a car, minivan, van, SUV, pick-up truck, or motorcycle with a gross vehicle weight rating of less than 14,000 pounds, and it must have undergone final assembly in the United States. The location of final assembly can be found on the vehicle information label or can be verified through the vehicle identification number (VIN).

Taxpayers can refer to the VIN Decoder website of the National Highway Traffic Safety Administration (NHTSA) for the plant of manufacture information to confirm if a vehicle was assembled in the United States.

Taxpayer Eligibility and Reporting Requirements

The deduction is accessible to both itemizing and non-itemizing taxpayers. When claiming the deduction, taxpayers must include the Vehicle Identification Number (VIN) of the qualified vehicle on their tax returns for the years in which deductions are claimed.

Lenders or recipients of qualified interest must file information returns with the IRS and provide statements to taxpayers detailing the total interest received during the taxable year. For tax year 2025, the IRS will offer transition relief regarding the new reporting requirements for interest recipients.

Enhanced Deduction for Seniors

Beginning with the Tax Year 2025, individuals aged 65 and older will have access to a new senior deduction of up to $6,000 per taxpayer. This initiative, introduced under the OBBBA, is a temporary measure that will be available for Tax Years 2025 through 2028.

This new deduction is in addition to the existing extra standard deduction available for seniors. To be eligible, taxpayers must be 65 or older by the last day of the tax year. Importantly, this senior deduction can be claimed regardless of whether the taxpayer chooses to itemize deductions or takes the standard deduction. It is also noteworthy that taxpayers do not need to be receiving Social Security benefits to qualify for this deduction.

For the Tax Year 2025, the Enhanced Deduction for Seniors will be reported on the new Schedule 1-A (Form 1040).

Eligibility for the new senior deduction is contingent upon meeting the following criteria:

- The taxpayer must be 65 or older by the end of the tax year.
- The taxpayer must possess a social security number valid for work in the U.S.

- The taxpayer must choose a filing status other than married filing separately.

Example:

For a single filer aged 65 and older in 2025:

- Base standard deduction: $15,750
- Existing additional deduction (for age 65+): $2,000
- New temporary senior deduction: Up to $6,000
- Total possible deduction: Up to $23,750

It is important to clarify a common misconception: the OBBBA does not exclude Social Security benefits from taxable income. However, the senior deduction is designed to assist in reducing tax liabilities for seniors, regardless of whether they are currently receiving Social Security benefits.

Charitable Contribution Deduction for Non-Itemizers

Effective in 2026, taxpayers who do not itemize their deductions will be able to claim a charitable contribution deduction. This provision makes permanent a temporary benefit that was previously available during the COVID relief years. The deduction is capped at:

- $1,000 for single filers
- $2,000 for joint filers

It is applicable only to cash contributions made to qualified charities and will likely be reported on Form 1040 or Schedule

A. This provision aims to encourage charitable giving among taxpayers who typically take the standard deduction. For instance, if you, as a single filer, donate $800 to a qualified charity, you can claim the full amount. In contrast, a married couple donating $3,000 can only deduct $2,000 due to the established cap.

Deductions applicable to individual taxpayers are reported on Schedule A and can include:

Medical and dental expenses can be deducted if they exceed 7.5% of your Adjusted Gross Income (AGI) and are not reimbursed. The IRS recognizes a variety of costs associated with the diagnosis, treatment, or prevention of diseases. Below is a breakdown of qualified expenses:

1. **Practitioners:**
   Fees for services rendered by medical professionals such as doctors, dentists, surgeons, chiropractors, psychiatrists, and psychologists are deductible.

2. **Dental Care:**
   Expenses for dental care, including cleanings, X-rays, fillings, braces, dentures, and oral surgeries, qualify for deduction.

3. **Vision & Hearing:**
   Costs for eye exams, prescription glasses, contact lenses, laser eye surgery, and hearing aids can also be deducted.

4. **Prescriptions:**
Only prescription medications and insulin are eligible for deduction. Generally, over-the-counter medications, except for insulin, do not qualify.

5. **Travel & Lodging:**
For medical travel, the mileage deduction is set at $0.21 per mile for 2025. Lodging expenses incurred while receiving medical care away from home can be deducted, up to a limit of $50 per night per person.

6. **Insurance Premiums:**
Premiums for medical and dental insurance that are paid with after-tax dollars (excluding amounts deducted through an employer's pre-tax plan) can be included.

7. **Long-Term Care:**
Costs for qualified long-term care services and certain insurance premiums also qualify for deduction.

However, there are non-deductible expenses to be aware of:

Cosmetic Surgery:
Typically, expenses for cosmetic procedures are not deductible unless they are necessary for treating a deformity related to an injury, disease, or congenital defect.

General Health:
Expenses for vitamins, gym memberships, diet foods, or vacations aimed at health improvement do not qualify.

Nicotine Products:
Non-prescription nicotine products, including gums and patches, are not deductible.

Toiletries:
Everyday items like toothpaste, cosmetics, and non-prescription mouthwash are also excluded from deductions.

Additionally, you may deduct medical expenses paid for:

- Yourself and your spouse,
- Dependents claimed on your tax return,
- Children of divorced or separated parents, regardless of whether they are claimed as dependents,
- Individuals you could have claimed as dependents were it not for their gross income exceeding $5,200 in 2025 or if they filed a joint return.

Understanding these details can help you better navigate and maximize your tax deductions related to medical and dental expenses.

Tax Deduction

When filing your taxes, it is important to understand the deductions available for state, local, and foreign taxes if you choose to itemize your deductions on Schedule A (Form 1040). There is an overall limit on the total deduction for state and local taxes.

Deductible Taxes (If You Itemize)

If you decide to itemize, you can generally deduct the following taxes paid during the year, as long as they are not associated with a business or rental activities:

State and Local Income Taxes or Sales Taxes:

You must select one option to deduct. Many taxpayers choose to deduct income taxes; however, in states without income tax or after making a large purchase, such as a vehicle, the sales tax deduction might be more advantageous. The IRS provides a Sales Tax Deduction Calculator to assist in this decision.

State and Local Real Property Taxes:
These taxes must be levied for general public welfare purposes, not for local benefits that would increase property value.

State and Local Personal Property Taxes:
You can deduct these only if they are based solely on the value of personal property and charged annually.

Foreign Income Taxes:
Taxes imposed by a foreign country or U.S. territory are typically deductible or can be credited against your tax liability.

Key Limitations
Itemizing Required: To take advantage of these deductions, you must itemize on Schedule A. You will need to compare the total of your itemized deductions with the standard deduction and select the higher amount.

SALT Cap:

The overall deduction for state and local taxes (SALT) has a limit. For tax returns in 2024, this limit is $10,000 (or $5,000 if married filing separately). For 2025 returns, the limit increases to $40,000 (or $20,000 if married filing separately), but it may be further reduced based on your Modified Adjusted Gross Income (MAGI).

Nondeductible Taxes

Certain taxes and fees are not deductible on Schedule A, including, but not limited to:

Federal income, Social Security, and Medicare taxes Federal excise taxes, Inheritance or estate taxes, Service charges for utilities such as water, sewer, or trash collection

For Self-Employed Individuals/Businesses

If you are self-employed, there are various taxes related to your business that can be deducted as business expenses on the appropriate forms (like Schedule C), separate from the itemized deductions. Understanding these deductions can help you optimize your tax filing process.

- Interest paid
- Charitable contributions
- Casualty and theft losses
- Other itemized deductions

There are also various miscellaneous deductions available, such as: Amortizable bond premiums, Federally or State declared Casualty and theft loss, Federal estate tax, Impairment-related work expenses, Claim repayments, Unrecovered pension investments, Schedule K-1, Ordinary loss on debt instruments, Standard deduction claimed with qualified disaster loss and Excess deduction on termination

This information is crucial for properly navigating tax obligations and maximizing available deductions and credits.

Miscellaneous itemized deductions

Miscellaneous itemized deductions have been permanently removed from the federal tax code, a change that originated with the Tax Cuts and Jobs Act (TCJA) of 2017 and was solidified by the One Big Beautiful Bill Act (OBBBA), which became law in July 2025. Prior to these changes, taxpayers could claim deductions for expenses that exceeded 2% of their adjusted gross income

(AGI). However, the repeal affects a broad range of expenses that are no longer deductible for most individuals. These include:

- Unreimbursed employee expenses such as per diem, travel, transportation, meal expenses, union dues, professional society dues, and work clothing or uniforms not suitable for everyday use.
- Investment-related expenses and fees, which encompass investment management fees, custodial fees, trustee fees for IRAs (if billed separately), and safe deposit box rental costs for storing investment documents.
- Tax preparation fees incurred for personal tax returns or tax software.
- Hobby expenses, which remain non-deductible even though any income generated is still taxable.
- Legal fees associated with non-business tax matters or personal job-related issues.

There are, however, a few exceptions for specific categories of employees who can still deduct unreimbursed expenses without being subject to the 2% AGI limitation. These categories include:

- Armed Forces reservists
- Qualified performing artists
- Fee-basis state or local government officials

Employees with impairment-related work expenses

Moreover, eligible educators can benefit from an above-the-line deduction for up to $300 of unreimbursed classroom expenses, representing an adjustment to income rather than an itemized deduction.

The consequence of eliminating these miscellaneous deductions is that most taxpayers now find it more advantageous to opt for the standard deduction, which has been significantly increased and made permanent by the OBBBA. For those who continue to itemize their deductions due to substantial mortgage interest or charitable contributions, the loss of these specific miscellaneous deductions means they no longer contribute to their total itemized deduction amounts.

Gambling Gains and Losses Deductions

Gains and losses from gambling activities can be a complex area for taxpayers and practitioners. Although gambling losses are generally not deductible, there are exceptions to this rule, particularly for professional gamblers.

A professional gambler can deduct all non-wagering expenses related to their gambling activities. This means that while wagering expenses are limited to gambling winnings, non-wagering expenses such as travel and research can be fully deducted. Consequently, a professional gambler who breaks even or incurs a net wagering loss may still benefit from deductible losses due to these additional expenditures.

It's essential to understand how wagering outlays affect gambling winnings. Net gambling winnings from transactions are included in the taxpayer's income, while deductions must be claimed on Schedule A. This distinction can lead to confusion. Gains from wagering are calculated on a transaction-by-transaction basis. For instance, a casual gambler should determine gross income from a wagering event by subtracting only the bets placed to achieve those winnings. These bets do not count as deductions in calculating adjusted gross income; they are merely part of the preliminary steps in assessing wagering gains.

Under Code section 165, taxpayers can take an itemized deduction limited to the amount of their wagering gains. For example, if a taxpayer places a $50 bet and wins $150 on a horse race, they have a $100 wagering gain (calculated as $150 won minus the $50 wager). If the taxpayer later loses $200 playing the lottery, they can use the Code section 165 deduction to offset the lottery loss. In this scenario, if the taxpayer itemizes their deductions, they can deduct $100 for the lottery loss (limited by their $100 wagering gain). Conversely, if the taxpayer does not itemize, the $100 in wagering gains would be included in their income without any offset for the loss.

Understanding these nuances can help taxpayers navigate the often confusing landscape of gambling deductions more effectively.

Understanding Income Tax:

Income tax is a crucial source of revenue for local, state, and federal governments, levied on individuals' income and businesses' profits. It's important to understand how income tax is calculated and the different types of taxable income. With various systems at the federal, state, and local levels, being aware of these differences can aid effective business and financial planning. Certain exemptions and deductions can help you save money, ultimately affecting the final taxable income.

Key Facts:

- Governments impose income tax on earnings from individuals and businesses to finance public services, social services, judicial systems, education, police, defense, and government functions.
- The U.S. has a progressive tax system, which means higher-income earners pay a larger share of their income in taxes.
- Individual income tax applies to wages and salaries, while business income tax is levied on corporations, independent contractors, and self-employed individuals.
- Nine states in the U.S. do not impose a state income tax, but they may collect other taxes such as sales tax, use taxes, real estate taxes, and personal property tax, and they might offer fewer public services.
- Tax credits and deductions can greatly reduce taxable income and total tax owed.

Americans simply do not pay taxes the claim that Americans simply do not pay taxes is a flat-out wrong notion. It's also not completely accurate to say that the bottom 50% of people in the United States don't pay taxes. In reality, the bottom half of taxpayers paid around 3.0% of the total federal income taxes collected, but this percentage can vary each year because of job losses or gains.

Here's an overview of the federal income tax status for the bottom 50% of U.S. taxpayers, based on 2022 data from the Tax Foundation.

1. **Average Tax Rate:**
   The bottom 50% paid an average federal income tax rate of 3.74%.
2. **Average Income Tax Paid:**
   They paid an average of $822 in federal income taxes.

3. **Income Range:**
   The income level that divides the top 50% from the bottom 50% was an Adjusted Gross Income (AGI) of $50,339.

Reasons Some People Pay Little or No Income Tax

While most people with income usually have a tax liability, some individuals may not owe any federal income taxes due to specific rules, such as filing status, dependents, standard deduction, and credits.

The most common reasons can contribute to this:

Standard Deduction:
Income below this threshold, defined by the standard deduction, is not subject to federal income tax and most state and local income taxes.

Tax Credits:
Various tax credits, including the Earned Income Tax Credit (EITC), Child Tax Credit, Child and Dependent Care Credit, Saver Credit, Education Credits, Foreign Tax Credit, and Adoption Credit, can significantly reduce a person's taxable income, sometimes bringing it to zero. In some cases, these credits can result in refunds that exceed the amount of taxes withheld.

Exempt Income:
Tax-exempt income refers to income that is not subject to federal, state, or local taxes. Although individuals and organizations may need to report this income on their tax returns, it will not be included when determining their tax liability.

It is important to note that these figures refer specifically to federal income tax. Most individuals, including those in the bottom 50%, still pay other taxes, such as:

- Payroll taxes, known as Social Security and Medicare.
- State and local income taxes are based on the standard deduction and where you reside.
- Sales taxes
- Homeowners pay property taxes either directly or indirectly through rent.

In other words, every American pays some type of tax, including those who receive welfare benefits. U.S. programs that can be considered welfare include Medicaid, Supplemental Security Income, the Supplemental Nutrition Assistance Program, the Children's Health Insurance Program, Temporary Assistance for Needy Families, housing assistance, and the Earned Income Tax Credit.

Understanding Taxpayers

Income earners are required to pay taxes on their earnings as they are received throughout the year, either through withholding or estimated payments. This means you are considered a taxpayer. If the tax withheld from your salary or pension is insufficient, or if you earn additional income from sources such as interest, dividends, alimony, self-employment income, capital gains, or winnings, you may need to make estimated tax payments. Self-employed individuals typically need to make these estimated payments as well. Estimated taxes cover not only income tax but also other taxes, such as self-employment tax and the alternative minimum tax.

Failing to pay enough tax through withholding and estimated payments could result in a penalty. You might also face penalties if your estimated payments are late, even if you're due a refund when you file your return.

Different rules apply to farmers, fishermen, and some higher-income taxpayers. Publication 505, Tax Withholding and Estimated Tax, provides more details on these special rules.

Qualified Business Income Deduction

The Qualified Business Income (QBI) deduction, introduced by the 2017 Tax Cuts and Jobs Act (TCJA), provides eligible self-employed individuals and small-business owners with the opportunity to claim an income deduction from their qualified trade or business. This deduction is also available to certain trusts and estates. The recent One Big Beautiful Bill Act (OBBBA) has made the QBI deduction a permanent feature of the tax code.

Known as Section 199A of the Internal Revenue Code, the QBI deduction allows eligible taxpayers, including owners of pass-through entities like partnerships, S corporations, and sole proprietorships, to deduct up to 20% of their QBI. In addition, taxpayers can also deduct up to 20% of qualified real estate investment trusts (REITs) dividends and income from publicly traded partnerships (PTPs), with some trusts and estates potentially qualifying as well.

Importantly, taxpayers can claim this deduction whether they opt for itemized deductions or the standard deduction, allowing for flexibility in tax planning. The deduction is taken at the owner, partner, or shareholder level rather than at the entity level for pass-through entities.

The QBI deduction consists of two primary components:

---

1. QBI Component: This component enables qualifying taxpayers to deduct 20% of their qualified business income stemming from a domestic business, irrespective of whether it operates as a sole proprietorship, S corporation, partnership, estate, or trust. The IRS defines qualified business income as the net amount of qualified items of income, gain, deduction, and loss from a qualified business or trade. However, there are several restrictions associated with this component, influenced by factors such as the nature of the trade or business, the total W-2 wages paid, and the unadjusted basis immediately after acquisition (UBIA) of the qualified property owned. Taxpayers who are patrons of horticultural or agricultural cooperatives may see a reduction in their QBI deduction due to these restrictions.

2. REIT or PTP Component: This component allows taxpayers to claim a deduction equivalent to 20% of the combined qualified REIT dividends—this includes dividends earned through a regulated investment company (RIC)—and income from qualified publicly traded partnerships (PTPs). Unlike the QBI component, the REIT or PTP component does not impose limitations based on W-2 wages or the unadjusted basis of qualified

property. Nevertheless, the amount of PTP income that qualifies may still be limited based on the taxpayer's income and the specific type of business in which the PTP is engaged.

"Understanding the QBI deduction can be beneficial for self-employed individuals and small business owners as they navigate their tax obligations and explore available deductions."

Understanding the Qualified Business Income (QBI) Deduction

The QBI deduction can provide significant tax relief for various business owners, including those operating partnerships, S corporations, sole proprietorships, single-member limited liability companies (LLCs), and certain trusts and estates. However, there are important limitations and qualifiers to be aware of.

Specified Service Trade or Business (SSTB)

One key consideration is whether the business qualifies as a specified service trade or business (SSTB). An SSTB may face limitations or the potential for elimination of its deduction based on the owner's taxable income. The IRS defines SSTBs to include those involved in health, law, accounting, actuarial science, performing arts, consulting, athletics, financial services, investment management, and others where the success is tied primarily to the reputation or skill of its employees or owners.

For SSTBs, the deduction for QBI is contingent upon the owner's total taxable income. As of 2025, the deduction begins to phase out when taxable income exceeds $394,600 for married couples filing jointly and $197,300 for other individual filers. The deduction is wholly eliminated when income surpasses $494,600 for married couples and $247,300 for other filers.

Non-SSTBs

For businesses that do not fall under the SSTB classification, if the owner's taxable income exceeds the designated thresholds, the QBI deduction may still be reduced. The deduction can be limited to the higher of the following two options:

1. 50% of the W-2 wages paid by the business.
2. 25% of the W-2 wages plus 2.5% of the unadjusted basis after acquisition (UBIA) of qualified property.

Qualified property refers to tangible assets used specifically in the operation of the trade or business.

Horticultural and Agricultural Cooperatives In certain situations, patrons of horticultural or agricultural cooperatives must also reduce their deduction according to section 199A(b)(7). Specifically, they must lower their cooperative QBI by the lesser of either of these amounts:

1. 9% of the qualified business income allocable to qualified payments.

2. 50% of the W-2 wages from the trade or business allocable to the qualified payments.

Exceptions to QBI

It is crucial to understand that not all income qualifies for the QBI deduction. The deduction is applicable only to income that is directly earned from a business and not merely on one's overall taxable income. The IRS outlines several types of income that are excluded from being classified as qualified business income, including:

Wage income

- Interest income not associated with a trade or business
- Investment-related items like capital gains or losses
- Income not effectively connected with business activities in the United States
- Annuities, unless received in connection with the trade or business
- Payments received by a partner for services rendered outside the capacity as a partner
- Certain dividends and payments in lieu of dividends
- Publicly traded partnership income
- Amounts received from a C corporation or as unreasonable compensation from an S corporation
- Understanding these parameters can help business owners effectively navigate the QBI deduction rules and maximize their potential tax benefits.

- Understanding the Calculation of the Qualified Business Income (QBI) Deduction

The Qualified Business Income (QBI) deduction plays a significant role in tax preparation for many taxpayers. While most tax preparation software can automate the calculation of this deduction, it's important for taxpayers to understand the key factors that determine eligibility for the full 20% deduction, a reduced deduction, or no deduction at all.

Here are the essential steps to consider:

1. Determine Business Type: First, identify whether the business qualifies as a specified service trade or business (SSTB). If it falls under this category, the total taxable income must be evaluated to assess eligibility for the full 20% deduction, a limited deduction, or none.

2. Assess Total Taxable Income: Next, calculate the taxpayer's total taxable income for the year. Regardless of the business type, if this income is below the specified threshold, the taxpayer is likely eligible for the full 20% QBI deduction.

3. Calculate Limited Deduction for SSTBs: If the business is classified as an SSTB and the taxable income is within the phase-in range, a limited deduction may apply. For the tax year 2024, this range is $383,900 to $483,900 for joint filers and $191,950 to $241,950 for other filers. In 2025, these thresholds will adjust to $197,300 for single taxpayers and $394,600 for joint filers.

4. Evaluate Competing Calculations: To determine the correct deduction amount, apply one of the following formulas:
    - Calculate 50% of the W-2 wages paid by the qualified trade or business, or
    - Calculate one-quarter (25%) of W-2 wages, plus 2.5% of the unadjusted basis immediately upon acquisition (UBIA) of qualified property.

After making these calculations, compare the results to 20% of the QBI and deduct the smaller amount."

"Given the complexity of these calculations, it's advisable to refer to the IRS instructions for Form 8995 for further guidance and assistance. Understanding these components can help ensure that taxpayers maximize their eligible deductions effectively."

Understanding the QBI Deduction Carryforward

A QBI (Qualified Business Income) deduction carryforward occurs when a business experiences negative QBI or qualified business losses, which can negatively affect the ability to claim the 20% deduction. These losses can be carried forward indefinitely until they are fully offset by positive qualified business income in future tax years.

According to the IRS, any negative QBI that is carried into the following tax year is classified as a qualified business net loss carryforward. This carryforward will be utilized in the subsequent year to determine the net qualified business income or loss for that year. If the net loss carryforward from the original year is not completely utilized in the following year, any remaining amount will then become a new qualified business net loss carryforward for application in the next tax year.

Reporting QBI Deduction

To report Qualified Business Income (QBI) deductions, taxpayers should utilize either Form 8995, which is designed for Simplified Computation, or Form 8995-A, which is the standard Qualified Business Income Deduction form.

If a taxpayer's taxable income exceeds the designated threshold or if their business is a patron of a specified cooperative, it is necessary to use Form 8995-A. Taxpayers with taxable income below the threshold may opt for Form 8995. Whichever form is appropriate must be attached to the tax return claiming the QBI deduction.

Recent changes under the Inflation Reduction Act (OBBBA) have affected the QBI deduction. The Act made the QBI deduction permanent and established a minimum deduction. Beginning in 2026, taxpayers with at least $1,000 in total QBI from an active qualified trade or business will be eligible for a minimum QBI deduction of $400. It's important to note that these figures will be adjusted for inflation starting in 2026.

Additionally, OBBBA raised the phase-in limitation ranges. Starting in 2026, these ranges will increase from $100,000 to $150,000 for joint filers and from $50,000 to $75,000 for other taxpayers.

For further information, consider visiting the OBBBA resource center, where you can find an executive summary of the Act, tips on advising clients, and more resources related to these legislative changes.

In 2026, various tax credits and savings programs implemented under the One Big Beautiful Bill Act (OBBBA) take effect, most notably the introduction of Trump Accounts. These new savings vehicles are designed for children and offer a tax-advantaged way to save.

Trump Accounts

Trump Accounts Overview (New for 2026)

Trump Accounts function similarly to custodial IRAs and are available to children under age 18.

- $1,000 Government Seed: Eligible U.S. citizen children born between January 1, 2025, and December 31, 2028, can receive a one-time $1,000 contribution from the U.S. Treasury.

- How to Claim: To set up a Trump Account and request the $1,000 contribution, authorized individuals must complete IRS Form 4547 with their 2025 tax return.

- Contribution Limits: After the initial contribution, annual contributions to the account are limited to $5,000, with inflation adjustments beginning in 2027.

- Online Enrollment: Enrollment for Trump Accounts is expected to start in mid-2026, and individuals can apply at trumpaccounts.gov.

  These measures aim to encourage savings and financial planning for future generations.

Who must pay estimated tax?

Individuals, including sole proprietors, self-employed workers, independent contractors, renters, partners in a partnership, S corporation shareholders, and some recipients of retirement payments who receive more than the standard deduction and did not have taxes withheld generally need to make estimated payments if they expect to owe at least $1,000 when filing. C corporations typically must pay estimated taxes if they expect to owe $500 or more.

You might need to pay estimated tax quarterly if your tax liability was more than zero last year. For details, see the worksheet in Form 1040-ES, Estimated Tax for Individuals.

Who does not need to pay estimated tax?

If you receive salaries and wages, you can avoid estimated payments by asking your employer to withhold more tax. To do this, file a new Form W-4 with your employer, specifying an additional amount to be withheld. For a pensioner, use Form W-4P, Withholding Certificate for Periodic Pension or Annuity Payment.

If you receive a paycheck, use the Tax Withholding Estimator to make sure the correct amount of tax is being withheld.

You don't need to pay estimated tax for the current year if:

- You had no tax liability last year.
- You were a U.S. citizen or resident alien all year.
- Your prior year covered a full 12 months.

If your total tax last year was zero or you didn't have to file, you also don't need to pay estimated tax.

How to figure out the estimated tax:

Individuals generally use Form 1040-ES, while nonresident aliens use Form 1040-ES(NR). To estimate your tax, determine your expected adjusted gross income, taxable income, taxes, deductions, and credits for the year.

Using last year's income, deductions, and credits as a guide is helpful. Complete the Form 1040-ES worksheet to estimate your tax. Adjust your estimates if your earnings are higher or lower than expected to avoid penalties. Update your estimates for changes in your situation or recent tax law developments.

When to pay estimated taxes:

The year is divided into four payment periods, known as quarters, each with a specific due date. First Quarter (Jan 1 - Mar 31 income): Last day to pay is April 15. Second Quarter (Apr 1 - May 31 income): Last day to pay is June 15. Third Quarter (Jun 1

- Aug 31 income): Last day to pay is September 15. Fourth Quarter (Sep 1 - Dec 31 income): Last day to pay is January 15 of the following year. Missing a payment may result in a penalty, even if you're eligible for a refund.

If mailing a payment, the postmark date is considered the payment date. Payments due on weekends or holidays are accepted if made on the next business day.

How to pay estimated taxes

Payments can be made through Form 1040-ES by mail, online, by phone, or via the IRS2Go app. You can also access your online account at IRS.gov/account to view payment history and records.

Businesses can pay most taxes, including estimated taxes, through their business tax account or Direct Pay. Some are required to use EFTPS.

You can choose to pay weekly, monthly, or at other intervals, as long as the total is paid by the end of the quarter. Visit IRS.gov/payments for options. Refer to Publication 505 for more details.

Penalty for underpayment

If you don't pay enough in taxes during the year, you might owe a penalty. Most taxpayers can avoid this if they owe less than $1,000 after withholding and credits, or if they pay at least 90% of this year's tax or 100% of last year's, whichever is less. Special rules apply to farmers, fishermen, and higher-income earners. See Publication 505 for details.

If your income fluctuates, you might avoid penalties by annualizing your income and making uneven payments. Use Form 2210 or 2220 to determine whether a penalty applies. Report any penalties on your return as instructed.

The penalty can be waived if:

- Extraordinary circumstances, such as a disaster, caused the underpayment.
- You retired or became disabled during the year, and the underpayment was due to reasonable cause rather than willful neglect.

How Income Taxes Are Collected

The Internal Revenue Service (IRS) is responsible for collecting taxes and enforcing tax laws nationwide. The IRS has detailed rules for reporting taxable income, deductions, credits, and business expenses. It collects taxes on all types of income, including wages, salaries, commissions, investment income, and business profits.

When you pay your individual income tax, you're not just giving money to the government — you're investing in vital programs that benefit the needy. Your contributions support important initiatives, including Welfare, Social Security, national defense, education, and infrastructure.

Business Income Tax:

Businesses, including self-employed individuals and independent contractors, are required to pay income tax on their profits after accounting for all expenses, deductions, and credits. The IRS taxes income from various entities, including corporations, partnerships, self-employed individuals, and small businesses. Depending on their business structure, businesses report their income and can deduct operating and capital expenses. The difference between gross income and these expenses usually represents taxable business income.

State and Local Income Tax

All but nine states in the U.S. do not impose individual income taxes. These states are Alaska, Florida, Nevada, New Hampshire,

South Dakota, Tennessee, Texas, Washington, and Wyoming. However, living in a state without an income tax may not always be cheaper overall. These states often compensate by levying other taxes or by offering fewer public services. Other factors also influence the cost of living, including healthcare, total expenses, and employment opportunities. For example, Florida residents face a 6% sales tax, while Tennessee's sales tax is 7%.

Fact Check:

If your tax situation is straightforward, a tax calculator can estimate your income tax liability. States often update their tax laws, making it hard to predict future tax burdens.

What Percent of Income Is Taxed? The portion of your income that is taxed, known as taxable income, depends on your earnings, filing status, deductions, and credits. Usually, higher incomes are taxed at higher rates. Federal rates range from 10% to 37%.

How Can I Calculate Income Tax? To find your income tax, add up all income for the year. Then calculate your adjusted gross income (AGI). Subtract eligible deductions and credits from your AGI to find your taxable income.

The Bottom Line:

All income earners are required to pay federal income tax, and many also pay state and local taxes, depending on their location. The United States uses a progressive tax system, meaning those who earn more pay higher rates. Deductions, exemptions, and credits can reduce taxable income and lower tax bills. Understanding federal and state tax systems helps taxpayers manage their taxes more effectively, and a tax calculator can estimate your income tax liability. States often revise their tax laws, making it difficult to predict future tax burdens.

Alternative Minimum Tax (AMT)

The Alternative Minimum Tax (AMT) is a distinct federal income tax framework established to ensure that high-income taxpayers contribute at least a minimum level of tax, even if they benefit from numerous deductions and credits available under the traditional tax system. Taxpayers who may be subject to the AMT are required to compute their tax liability twice—once according to standard tax rules and once according to AMT guidelines—paying the higher amount.

How the AMT Works

The AMT calculation usually involves adding back certain tax benefits, such as the standard deduction or deductions for state and local taxes (SALT), to the regular taxable income. This adjusted figure is known as Alternative Minimum Taxable Income (AMTI). From the AMTI, taxpayers can subtract an AMT exemption amount, provided their income falls below the phase out threshold. The remaining taxable income is then taxed at one of two AMT rates.

Key Insights

Purpose: The AMT was introduced in 1969 to curb the ability of wealthy individuals to exploit loopholes that allowed them to evade paying income taxes.

Who Pays: The AMT primarily affects high-income taxpayers with substantial itemized deductions, significant capital gains, or those who exercise incentive stock options (ISOs).

- Rates: The AMT employs two tax rates: 26% and 28%, which generally fall below the highest regular income tax rate of 37%.
- Recent Changes: The 2017 Tax Cuts and Jobs Act (TCJA) notably decreased the number of taxpayers subjected to the AMT by raising exemption and phaseout thresholds. However, the "One Big Beautiful Bill Act" (OBBBA) enacted in 2025 made the higher exemptions permanent while introducing accelerated phaseout rules starting in 2026, potentially bringing more high-income taxpayers back into the AMT.

"For official information and to assess whether you might be impacted by this tax, refer to the instructions for IRS Form 1040 and complete IRS Form 6251."

Excise Tax on Remittance Transfers

Starting in 2026, a 1% excise tax will be imposed on remittance transfers, which include cash transactions sent from the U.S. to locations abroad. This applies to various forms of money transfers, such as:

- Money orders
- Cashier's checks
- Cash

The purpose of this tax is to generate revenue and enhance reporting transparency regarding outbound financial transfers. For example, if Carlos sends $5,000 to his family overseas using a money order, he will be responsible for a $50 excise tax. Similarly, if Roxanne sends $1,000 via a cashier's check, she will owe $10 in excise tax.

What is 1040 Tax Form

Importance of the 1040 Form

Form 1040 is a document that U.S. individuals, sole proprietors, independent contractors, and owners of single-member LLCs use to report business income and expenses as part of their personal tax return. Taxpayers file it with the Internal Revenue Service (IRS) to report annual income tax returns. It summarizes a taxpayer's income, deductions, and credits, helping determine their overall tax liability or potential refund for the year. Form 1040 is specifically designed for U.S. taxpayers to file yearly income tax returns. For taxpayers aged 65 or older, Form 1040-SR is available as an optional alternative; it follows the same schedules and instructions as Form 1040.

This 1040 form collects details about your income, deductions, credits, and tax payments to determine whether you owe additional taxes or qualify for a refund. By understanding the different sections and schedules of the 1040 form, you can report your financial information more accurately and may improve your tax outcomes.

You might need to report Additional Income and Adjustments to Income on SCHEDULE 1, such as unemployment compensation, prize or award money, and gambling winnings.

They can also claim deductions like student loan interest, self-employment tax, and educator expenses. Additionally, they may owe other taxes, including self-employment tax, household employment taxes, or extra taxes on IRAs and other qualified retirement plans. If an excess advance premium tax credit repayment is required, it should also be reported.

Taxpayers may claim credits that they haven't previously claimed on Form 1040 or 1040-SR, such as the foreign tax credit, education credits, and the general business credit. Other payments, including amounts paid with a request for an extension to file or excess Social Security tax withheld, can also be reported.

Taxpayers can calculate their deductions and determine how much they owe to the IRS. If you are a U.S. resident and meet certain criteria, filling out Form 1040 is required.

Commonly required attachments for Form 1040 include Schedule 1, Schedule 2, Schedule 3, and Schedule A, which is only used for itemized deductions. Additionally, there may be other schedules or forms needed for specific taxpayers. If these do not apply to you, you may not need them.

Schedule B Interest and Ordinary Dividends

This document is intended for individual taxpayers who need to report interest and ordinary dividend income. You are generally required to file this form if your total taxable interest or ordinary dividends exceed $1,500 for the year. Additionally, it's necessary to file this form if you meet any of the following criteria:

- You received interest from a seller-financed mortgage.
- You are claiming an exclusion for interest earned from Series EE or I U.S. savings bonds.
- You had a financial interest in, or signature authority over, a financial account located in a foreign country, or you received a distribution from a foreign trust.

To complete this form accurately, you will typically need information from Forms 1099-INT and 1099-DIV provided by your financial institutions.

Schedule C: Overview of Filing Requirements

Schedule C is a tax form that individuals typically complete if they engage in activities primarily intended to generate profit on a regular, consistent basis. The following are common categories of filers who often need to submit this form:

- Sole Proprietors: These are unincorporated business owners who operate their businesses independently and are the sole owners of their ventures.
- Independent Contractors & Freelancers: Individuals who receive a Form 1099-NEC, which indicates non-employee compensation, fall into this category.
- Single-Member LLCs: Limited Liability Companies with only one owner that have not chosen to be taxed as corporations are also required to file this form.

- Statutory Employees: These are workers who have Social Security and Medicare taxes withheld from their pay but are otherwise treated as self-employed for tax purposes.

Understanding these classifications can help individuals determine their responsibilities regarding Schedule C filings.

Schedule D: Reporting Capital Gains and Losses

Schedule D is an IRS tax form that individuals use to report capital gains and losses from the sale or trade of specific properties or investments, including stocks, bonds, real estate, and digital assets. This schedule is typically attached to the primary income tax return, such as Form 1040.

The key functions of Schedule D include:

1. Calculating Overall Gain or Loss: It helps determine the total profit or loss resulting from transactions involving capital assets.
2. Determining Tax Liability: It calculates the tax owed on capital gains, which may be subject to different tax rates based on the holding period of the asset (short-term vs. long-term).
3. Deducting Capital Losses: You can deduct capital losses against capital gains, and potentially against a limited amount of ordinary income (up to $3,000 for single filers, or $1,500 if married filing separately).
4. Reporting Capital Loss Carryovers: It allows you to report any capital loss carryovers from prior tax years.

Key Information Needed

When completing Schedule D, it's important to gather the following information for each transaction:

- A description of the property (e.g., number of shares, company name, address and EIN number).
- Dates of acquisition and sale.
- Sale price (proceeds).
- Cost or other basis (your initial investment amount, including commissions and fees).
- Any applicable adjustments to gain or loss.

Filing in Conjunction with Form 8949

Typically, before completing Schedule D, you will need to fill out Form 8949, which is used to detail each individual transaction involving the sale of capital assets. The totals from Form 8949 are then transferred to Schedule D, where the overall capital gain or loss is summarized.

In some cases, you may not need to file Form 8949 if your broker has reported the cost basis to the IRS on Form 1099-B and there are no adjustments to either the basis or the type of gain or loss.

Securities

Overview of Capital Gains and Losses

Understanding the rules related to capital gains and losses is essential for most investors, although it's important to note that securities dealers and day traders may use different accounting methods for their transactions.

Basis of Stocks and Bonds

When purchasing stocks or bonds, the basis is generally determined by the purchase price in addition to any associated costs, such as commissions and transfer fees.

Nontaxable Stock Dividends and Stock Splits

In cases of nontaxable stock dividends or stock splits, the shareholder's percentage of ownership remains unchanged. To allocate the total adjustsed basis of all shares, it is done pro-rata to each share. The basis of existing shares must be reduced by the amount allocated to the new shares, and this rule only applies when the additional stock received is the same type as the stock already held.

Return of Capital

Return of capital, also known as non-dividend distributions, refers to amounts that reduce the basis of the investment.

Identifying Shares and Reporting Transactions

When an investor engages in multiple transactions at different times and in varying quantities without being able to identify the specific shares sold, the basis applied will follow the first-in, first-out (FIFO) method, meaning the oldest shares are considered sold first. However, if the taxpayer can adequately identify the shares sold, they may report those specific shares regardless of any purchase order.

Reporting Capital Gains and Losses Calculating Net Capital Gain or Loss

---

Upon selling a capital asset, the capital gain or loss is determined by the difference between the adjusted basis of the asset and the sale amount. A capital gain occurs if the asset sells for more than the adjusted basis, whereas a capital loss occurs if it sells for less.

To effectively calculate the net capital gain or loss, it's crucial to categorize capital gains and losses as either long-term or short-term. Gains and losses within each category should be combined to derive a net gain or loss.

Short-Term Gains and Losses

Short-term capital gains and losses arise from the sale or trade of investment property held for one year or less. This includes any short-term capital gain or loss from partnerships, S corporations, fiduciaries, as well as any short-term capital loss carryover, which should be combined to determine net short-term capital gain (NSTCG) or loss (NSTCL).

Long-Term Gains and Losses

Long-term capital gains and losses occur from the sale of investment property held for more than one year. Similar to short-term transactions, the taxpayer's share from partnerships, S corporations, and fiduciaries, along with long-term capital loss carryovers, should be combined to arrive at a net long-term capital gain (NLTCG) or loss (NLTCL).

Total Net Gain or Loss

To calculate total net gain or loss, taxpayers compare their net short-term capital results to their net long-term capital results. The character of the resulting gain or loss depends on which of the two is larger:

- If both types of capital results are present (e.g., net long-term capital gains and net short-term capital losses), the resulting tax character follows that of the larger amount. For instance, if short-term losses exceed long-term gains, the overall loss will be characterized as short-term.
- Conversely, if long-term gains surpass short-term losses, the resulting gain is long-term and is subject to the maximum capital gain tax rates.

  Each loss maintains its respective character, whether short-term or long-term, and the same applies to gains. Short-term gains are taxed at ordinary income tax rates, while long-term gains benefit from the lower maximum net capital gain tax rates.

Conclusion on Net Capital Gains

Net capital gains typically receive advantageous tax treatment compared to ordinary gains, which are taxed at higher ordinary income tax rates. This can lead to lower overall tax liabilities for those realizing gains from long-term capital assets.

What is the maximum capital gain rate?

When it comes to capital gains tax, it's important to understand the different rates that apply depending on the type of gain and your filing status. Here's a breakdown:

1. **Types of Capital Gains and Their Rates:**

    - Collectibles or Qualified Small Business Stock: Gains are taxed at a maximum rate of 28%.
    - Unrecaptured Section 1250 Gain: This type of gain is taxed at a maximum rate of 25%.
    - All Other Capital Gains: Generally subject to a maximum rate of 20%.

Long-term capital gains, which exclude those from collectibles, qualified small business stock, or unrecaptured Section 1250 gains, benefit from lower tax rates compared to short-term capital gains, which are taxed as ordinary income. For non-corporate taxpayers, net long-term capital gains are typically taxed at a maximum rate of 20%.

2. **Special Considerations:**

Reduced maximum rates may apply to long-term capital gains from stocks and bonds (excluding qualified small business stock) as well as certain real property transactions.

3. **Capital Gain Rates by Filing Status:**

The following table outlines the maximum amounts for zero and 15% tax rates based on your filing status:

- Married Filing Joint and Qualifying Surviving Spouse:
- Maximum Zero Rate Amount: $96,700
- Maximum 15% Rate Amount: $600,050
- Married Filing Separate:
- Maximum Zero Rate Amount: $48,350
- Maximum 15% Rate Amount: $300,000

4. **Head of Household:**
   - Maximum Zero Rate Amount: $64,750
   - Maximum 15% Rate Amount: $566,700
5. **Other Individuals:**
   - Maximum Zero Rate Amount: $48,350
   - Maximum 15% Rate Amount: $533,400

For individuals with an adjusted net capital gain, if the gain does not result in taxable income exceeding the maximum zero rate amount, it is not taxed. If the gain results in taxable income exceeding the zero rate but not exceeding the maximum 15% rate amount, it is taxed at 15%. Any remaining adjusted net capital gain is then taxed at 20%.

It's also important to note that net short-term capital gains are taxed at ordinary income rates. Understanding these nuances can help in planning and optimizing your tax situation.

Net Capital Loss

An individual with an adjusted net capital loss can deduct the lesser of:

- $3,000 ($1,500 if married filing separately)
- Total net capital loss (from Schedule D)
- Taxable income before the net capital loss.

A net capital loss can reduce income dollar for dollar up to the $3,000 limit. Any unused portion can be carried over to future years indefinitely. Losses cannot be carried back to prior years.

Capital Loss Carryover

When calculating the capital loss carryover, consider the current year's allowable deduction. It retains its nature (long-term or short-term) when carried over. Use short-term losses first, followed by long-term losses, until the deduction limit is reached.

Example: Tom's 2025 net Short-Term Capital Loss is $5,000, and his net Long-Term Capital Loss is $10,000. He can deduct $3,000, using short-term losses first, and carry forward $2,000 of Short-Term Capital Loss and $10,000 of LTCL to 2026.

TIP: A decedent's capital loss can only be deducted on their final tax return. Carryovers do not transfer to an estate or surviving spouse. Joint filers should consider recognizing capital gains to utilize any capital loss carryforward.

Reporting

Brokers must file Form 1099-B for each person for whom they sold securities or exchanged property. Taxpayers use Form 8949 to report capital gain and loss transactions, transferring subtotals to Schedule D (Form 1040).

Form 8949 is for detailed reporting of short-term and long-term transactions, categorized into three classes based on whether the basis was reported. Short-term transactions are listed in Part I and long-term in Part II.

Schedule D summarizes the overall capital gain or loss. If only reporting capital gain distributions, report directly on Form 1040 without Schedule D.

Schedule E (Form 1040) Overview

Schedule E (Form 1040) is an important IRS tax form utilized by individual taxpayers to report supplemental income and losses derived from passive activities. This form is submitted along with the main Form 1040 tax return, making it essential for declaring income sources beyond traditional wages or active business revenue.

Sections of Schedule E

Schedule E is organized into several parts, each addressing specific types of income. Taxpayers should complete only the sections relevant to their financial situation:

- **Part I:** Focuses on income or loss from rental real estate and royalties, which may include earnings from oil, gas, mineral, or intellectual property royalties.
- **Part II:** Pertains to income or loss from partnerships and S corporations, based on the information provided via a Schedule K-1.
- **Part III:** Covers income or loss from estates and trusts, also reliant on a Schedule K-1.
- **Part IV:** Addresses income or loss from real estate mortgage investment conduits (REMICs).
- **Part V:** Summarizes the totals from the previous parts.

Key Considerations for Rental Properties

For most landlords, Part I of Schedule E is particularly significant. Here, individuals report gross rental income and may deduct ordinary and necessary expenses related to managing their rental properties. Common deductible expenses include:

- Advertising costs
- Auto and travel expenses related to the property (using actual expenses or the standard mileage rate)
- Cleaning and maintenance expenses
- Insurance premiums

- Legal and professional fees (such as tax preparation and property management)
- Mortgage interest (only the interest portion, not the principal)
- Repair costs (excluding major improvements, which must be depreciated)
- Property taxes
- Utilities (if covered by the landlord)
- Depreciation (applicable to the building, not the land)

Distinguishing Between Schedule E and Schedule C

The primary distinction between Schedule E and Schedule C lies in the level of involvement and the services provided by the taxpayer:

- Schedule E is used for passive rental activities, such as standard long-term leases, where only basic services (like heating, lighting, and trash removal) are provided.
- Schedule C is appropriate for rental activities treated as a business, such as operating a hotel or short-term vacation rentals (like Airbnb or VRBO), where significant services (like daily cleaning, meals, or concierge services) are offered.

Common Applications for Schedule E

The form is used to report income or loss from various sources, including:

1. Rental Real Estate: Income from leasing properties to tenants.
2. Royalties: Payments from properties involving oil, gas, minerals, or intellectual property rights such as copyrights and patents.
3. Pass-Through Entities: Shares of income, expenses, and credits from partnerships and S corporations, usually reflected on a Schedule K-1.
4. Estates and Trusts: Income received as a beneficiary.
5. REMICs: Involvement in residual interests within real estate mortgage investment conduits.

Important Filing Information

When preparing Schedule E, several key points should be noted:

1. **Passive vs. Active Income:**
   Generally, income reported on Schedule E is treated as "passive." Thus, it may be subject to Passive Activity Loss rules, which can limit the deductibility of losses against other income.

2. **Deductible Expenses:**
   Rental property owners can deduct allowable "ordinary and necessary" expenses such as mortgage interest, property taxes, repairs, insurance, management fees, and depreciation.

3. **Substantial Services:**
   If significant services are provided (like daily cleaning or meals in a bed-and-breakfast), the taxpayer is typically required to file Schedule C instead of Schedule E.

4. **Deadlines:**
   Schedule E must be filed as part of Form 1040 and is due by April 15, with the option to extend the deadline to October 15 if needed.

Understanding the Basis of Property

Cost Basis

The basis of property refers to a taxpayer's investment in that property for tax purposes. To determine a gain or loss, one must subtract the adjusted basis from the proceeds obtained from the sale, exchange, or other disposition of the property. The basis is crucial for calculating deductions related to depreciation, amortization, depletion, and casualty losses.

When a taxpayer utilizes property for both business (or investment) and personal purposes, it is essential to allocate the basis appropriately according to each use. Only the portion of the basis assigned to business or investment use is eligible for depreciation.

Typically, the basis of a property is its cost, which includes all amounts paid in cash, debt obligations, or in the form of other property or services. The cost basis may also encompass various additional costs, such as:

5. Commissions
6. Sales tax, freight, installation, and testing fees
7. Legal and accounting fees that must be capitalized
8. Excise taxes, revenue stamps, recording fees, and real estate taxes if assuming the seller's liability

The original basis of a property can be modified through specific events, such as:

- Improvements to a property, which will increase the basis
- Deductions for depreciation, casualty losses, or the claiming of certain credits, which will reduce the basis

Real Property

Real property, often referred to as real estate, includes land and any structures, vegetation, or attachments on that land. When a taxpayer purchases both buildings and the land they occupy for a single price, it is important to allocate the cost basis between the land and the buildings. This allocation should be based on the respective fair market values (FMV) of both at the time of purchase.

The basis for each asset can be calculated by taking a fraction of the lump sum paid: the numerator being the FMV of the specific asset and the denominator being the FMV of the entire property package at the time of purchase.

Important Note: Land is not subject to depreciation; therefore, taxpayers must allocate a portion of the purchase price to land before determining the depreciation deduction for buildings or structures. Additionally, improvements enhancing the value of a building do not affect the basis of the land.

When acquiring property with an existing mortgage, the basis will include the purchase price plus any amounts that will be paid on the mortgage. Basis adjustments may also occur due to specific settlement costs, including:

- Settlement fees and closing costs associated with purchasing the property (note that costs related to financing, such as loan fees, should not be included in the basis)
    - Abstract fees (title abstract fees)
    - Charges for utility service installations
    - Legal fees for title searches, sales contracts, and deed preparation
    - Recording and survey fees
    - Transfer taxes
    - Owner's title insurance

- Any amounts the buyer agrees to pay on behalf of the seller, such as back taxes, interest, recording or mortgage fees, costs for improvements or repairs, and sales commissions

  Understanding these components is essential for accurate tax reporting and property management.

Taxpayers cannot add the following settlement fees and closing costs to the basis of a property:

1. Casualty insurance premiums
2. Rent for occupancy of the property before closing
3. Charges for utilities or services related to the property before closing
4. Loan-related charges, including points (discount points and loan origination fees), mortgage insurance

premiums, loan assumption fees, costs of a credit report, and fees for appraisals required by a lender

5. Fees for refinancing a mortgage If a taxpayer pays points to secure a loan (including a mortgage, second mortgage, line of credit, or home equity loan), these points may not be added to the basis of the property. Instead, the taxpayer will generally deduct these points over the term of the loan.

Additionally, amounts placed in escrow for future payment of taxes and insurance cannot be included in the basis.

Important: The term "points" refers to certain charges paid to obtain a home mortgage. Points are considered prepaid interest and may qualify for deduction as home mortgage interest. Special rules apply to points paid on a mortgage for a primary residence. If certain requirements are met, a taxpayer may deduct the points in full in the year they are paid. Points paid for refinancing, however, are generally only deductible over the life of the new mortgage. Points do not increase the basis of the property.

Points charged for specific services, such as preparation costs for a mortgage note, appraisal fees, or notary fees, are not classified as interest and cannot be deducted. Points paid by the seller of a home cannot be deducted as interest on the seller's return, but they do qualify as a selling expense that reduces the amount of gain realized. Conversely, points paid by the seller can be deducted by the buyer, provided the buyer subtracts the amount from the basis (or cost) of the residence. Points paid on loans secured by a second home can be deducted only over the life of that loan.

Adjusted Basis

Before calculating any gain or loss from the sale, exchange, or disposition of property, as well as determining allowable depreciation, depletion, or amortization, it is essential for taxpayers to adjust the cost of the property accordingly. This process results in what is known as the adjusted basis.

To increase the basis of any property, taxpayers should consider all items that can be properly added to a capital account. These items include:

Capital Improvements: Costs incurred for enhancements that have a useful life extending beyond one year and either increase the property's value, extend its lifespan, or adapt it for a different use. Examples of capital improvements include:

1. Constructing a recreation room in an unfinished basement
2. Adding an extra bathroom or bedroom
3. Building a fence
4. Installing new plumbing or wiring
5. Putting on a new roof
6. Paving the driveway

Assessments for Local Improvements: Property assessments associated with improvements that enhance the property's value should be added to the basis. These assessments cannot be deducted as taxes and may include:

- Road construction
- Sidewalk installations
- Water connections

- Extending utility service lines to the property

Conversely, the basis of any property must be decreased by any items representing a return of capital during the period the taxpayer held the property. Notable examples include:

Non-Taxable Corporate Distributions: Also referred to as non-dividend distributions, these amounts reflect a return of capital and therefore reduce the basis.

Casualty and Theft Losses:

The basis should be decreased by any insurance proceeds received or other reimbursements, as well as by any deductible loss not covered by insurance. Conversely, if repairs are made to restore the property to its pre-casualty condition, the basis should be increased by those repair costs.

1. **Depreciation and Section 179 Deductions:**
   The basis of qualifying business property will be lowered by any Section 179 deductions claimed, along with the depreciation deducted (or that could have been deducted) according to the taxpayer's chosen method of depreciation.
2. **Easements:**
   Generally, if compensation is received for granting an easement, it is treated by the IRS as proceeds from the sale of a real property interest, necessitating a reduction in the property's basis by the amount received.

3. **Certain Credits:**
   The basis may also be reduced by the amount of credits received for specific items, such as:
   - Alternative motor vehicle credit
   - Alternative fuel vehicle refueling property credit
   - Residential energy-efficient property credit

   Understanding these adjustments is crucial for accurately determining the adjusted basis and managing tax implications effectively.

Property Received for Services

When a taxpayer receives property in exchange for services rendered, the fair market value (FMV) of that property must be included in their income. This FMV then serves as the basis for the property. If the taxpayer and the payer agreed on a price beforehand, the IRS typically accepts this agreed price as the FMV, provided there is no contrary evidence.

In cases where the property is subject to specific restrictions, the basis is generally determined based on its FMV at the time it substantially vests. However, this rule does not apply if the taxpayer elects to report the FMV of the property at the time of transfer, subtracting any amount they may have paid for it.

Property is considered to be substantially vested when it can be transferred freely or is not at risk of substantial forfeiture, meaning the taxpayer has little chance of losing it.

Bargain Purchases

A bargain purchase occurs when an item is acquired for less than its fair market value (FMV). If a taxpayer purchases goods or property for less than FMV as compensation for services, the difference between the purchase price and the FMV must be reported as income. In this case, the property's basis is considered to be its FMV, which includes the purchase price plus any amount included as income.

Involuntary Conversions

When a taxpayer receives replacement property due to an involuntary conversion—such as a casualty, theft, or condemnation—the basis of the replacement property is determined based on the basis of the original property that was converted.

1. **Similar or Related Property:** If the replacement property is similar or related in service or use to the converted property, its basis is the same as the original property's basis at the time of conversion, with specific adjustments:
   - Decrease the basis by any recognized loss from the involuntary conversion and any cash received that is not reinvested in similar property.
   - Increase the basis by any recognized gain from the conversion and any costs incurred in acquiring the replacement property.
2. **Money or Property Not Similar or Related:**
   If the taxpayer receives cash or property that is not similar to the converted property and subsequently purchases similar property, the basis of the new property will be its cost, reduced by any gain that was not recognized during the conversion.

   Example: John's dog accidentally damages his work laptop, valued at $2,000. He receives a $2,500 insurance reimbursement and buys a new laptop for $2,200. Since John recognizes a gain of $500, his basis in the new laptop increases. However, because he does not use $300 of the proceeds to reinvest, this reduces his basis. Thus, the adjusted basis for the new laptop is $1,900 ($2,200 - $300).

Property Received as a Gift

Determining the basis of property received as a gift involves knowing the donor's adjusted basis, the property's FMV at the time of the gift, and any gift tax that was paid. The relationship between the FMV and the donor's basis dictates the applicable rule:

- If the donor's adjusted basis sets the basis for the taxpayer, the IRS treats the holding period as beginning on the same day the donor's holding period commenced.
- If the FMV determines the basis, the taxpayer's holding period starts the day after the gift is made.

3. **When FMV is Less than Donor's Adjusted Basis:** The basis will differ based on whether a gain or loss occurs upon the sale of the property:
   - To calculate gain, the basis is the donor's adjusted basis.
   - To calculate loss, the basis is the FMV at the time the gift was received.

When FMV is Equal to or Greater than Donor's Adjusted Basis: The basis is the donor's adjusted basis at the time of the gift. If the donor paid gift tax, the basis is increased by the portion of the gift tax attributable to the net increase in the gift's value, determined by the formula:

- Gift tax paid × (FMV - Donor's adjusted basis) / FMV.

Property Transferred from a Spouse

When property is transferred from a taxpayer's spouse or a former spouse as part of a divorce settlement, the basis and holding period for the recipient remain the same as the spouse's adjusted basis. Taxpayers do not recognize any gain or loss from the transfer of property between spouses or ex-spouses during divorce, which holds true even when cash or other forms of compensation are involved.

Inherited Property Overview

When dealing with inherited property, it's important to note that, with the exception of certain transfers made in 2010 that opted for a modified carryover basis, any gain realized is categorized as long-term. The basis for inherited capital assets is typically determined by the fair market value (FMV) at the time of the decedent's death, or at an alternate valuation date if chosen by the personal representative of the estate. This process, known as a step-up in basis, occurs when the FMV is higher than what the decedent's original basis was.

Forms of Ownership and Their Impact on Step-Up

---

1. **Qualified Joint Interest:**
   This refers to a property owned by a married couple as tenants by the entirety or as tenants with rights of

survivorship. In this case, half of the property's value receives a step-up in basis to its FMV.

2. **Joint Tenancy with Rights of Survivorship (JTWROS):** Under this arrangement, joint tenants share an equal interest in the property. If one owner passes away, only the portion of the property that is included in the decedent's estate receives a step-up in basis. The percentage eligible for the step-up is influenced by the amount of the property that the decedent contributed versus any gifts made. For instance, if a decedent contributed 75% to the property's total value and did not gift any part of it, then 75% of that property would receive a step-up in basis.
3. **Community Property:**
In states that follow community property laws—such as Arizona, California, Idaho, Louisiana, Nevada, New Mexico, Texas, Washington, and Wisconsin—both spouses generally own an equal share of the community property. Upon the death of one spouse, the total value of all community property, including the share belonging to the surviving spouse, may receive a step-up in basis, as long as the deceased spouse's portion is included in their gross estate.

Transitioning Property from Personal to Business Use

When property initially held for personal use is converted to business use or rental purposes, the taxpayer may begin to depreciate it at the time of this change. To accurately calculate the basis for depreciation, consider the lesser of the following values:

- The FMV of the property on the date of conversion
- The adjusted basis on the date of conversion

If the taxpayer sells the property at a loss, the FMV at the time of conversion (with necessary adjustments) will be considered for determining the basis. Conversely, if the property is sold at a profit, the original adjusted basis will be used. This guideline is designed to prevent taxpayers from converting non-deductible losses related to personal property into deductible losses associated with business property.

Rental Income and Expenses

Several key factors influence the amount of rental income that a taxpayer must report on their tax return. The IRS permits specific expenses to be deducted from gross rental income, which can result in either a gain or a loss from rental activities. Taxpayers should report their gross rental income and expenses on Schedule E, subsequently transferring the net income or allowable loss to Form 1040.

Personal Use Property

The IRS categorizes rental real estate as a personal residence if it is utilized for personal purposes for more than either 14 days or 10% of the total days it is rented out.

For properties not classified as personal residences, taxpayers should report all rental income and deduct all associated rental expenses, which may exceed the gross rental income. Conversely, if the property is used as a home, the rental income and deductions will depend on the duration for which it was rented at fair market value.

- If the property is rented for fewer than 15 days within a year, it is not considered rental activity. In this case, taxpayers do not include any rental income or deduct any rental expenses.
- If rented for 15 days or more, taxpayers must report the entire rental income and allocate expenses between rental and personal use. If this results in a loss, it's important to note that not all expenses may be deductible.

"Personal use" refers to days the owner or family members occupy the property or when the property is used for less than fair value. However, any day the taxpayer rents the unit at a fair rental price, even if it's used for personal purposes that day, counts as a rental use day. Conversely, days the property is available but not rented do not qualify as rental use.

Rental Income

Typically, taxpayers are required to include all amounts received as rent in their gross income. Rental income encompasses any payments made for the use or occupation of property. In addition to standard rent payments, other forms of income may also qualify as rental income.

1. **Advance Rent:**
   Any payment received before the rental period it covers should be included in rental income for the year received, irrespective of the period it spans or the accounting method used.
2. **Security Deposits:**
   A security deposit should not be recognized as income when initially received, provided it is refundable to the tenant at the lease's conclusion. However, if a portion or the entirety of the deposit is kept due to a tenant's breach of lease terms, that amount must be reported as income in the year it is retained. Any amount designated as a security deposit but treated as final rent payment should be considered advance rent and included in income upon receipt.
3. **Expenses Paid by Tenant:**
   If a tenant covers any expenses that are normally the landlord's responsibility, these amounts must also be reported as rental income and are eligible for certain deductible expenses.

4. **Property or Services:**
   When rent is received in the form of property or services rather than cash, the fair market value of these as rental income should be included. If the services are provided at an agreed-upon rate, this is usually regarded as the fair market value.

Rents from Personal Property

When renting out personal items such as equipment or vehicles, the approach to reporting income and expenses hinges on whether the rental activity is conducted as a business meant for profit. Generally, if the primary objective is income generation and the taxpayer is regularly engaged in the rental business, it qualifies as a business. In such cases, income and expenses should be reported on Schedule C. If the rental activity does not qualify as a business, report the rental income as "other income" on Form 1040, with any associated expenses listed as an adjustment to gross income.

Rental Expenses

Related Expenses

When it comes to rental income, various expenses can be deducted to help reduce taxable income. These include advertising costs, cleaning and maintenance expenses, utilities, property taxes, interest, commissions related to rent collection, as well as travel and transportation costs associated with rental activities.

Fire and Liability Insurance

For insurance premiums paid in advance for multiple years, only the portion that applies to future years can be deducted in those respective years. Therefore, taxpayers cannot deduct the entire premium in the year it was initially paid.

Depreciation

Depreciation allows property owners to recover the cost of their rental property through annual tax deductions, but it only applies when the property is ready and available for rent. The recovery period varies based on property type: residential rental properties can be depreciated over 27.5 years, while nonresidential properties are depreciated over 39 years. It's important to note that land costs are not subject to depreciation.

Repairs

Expenses incurred for repairs are deductible as they keep the property in good working condition without significantly adding to its value or extending its life. Examples include repainting, fixing gutters, and repairing leaks or broken windows. However, if repairs are part of a larger remodeling project that improves the property, those costs are considered improvements and cannot be deducted directly. Instead, they must be capitalized and depreciated.

Improvements

Improvements, which enhance the value of a property, extend its useful life, or adapt it for new uses, must be capitalized. Examples of improvements include adding a bathroom, building a fence, or installing new plumbing. Unlike repairs, the costs associated with improvements cannot be directly deducted in the year they are incurred.

Additional Considerations

Local benefit taxes, which result from enhancements to property value such as new streets or sidewalks, are generally not deductible. Instead, these charges are treated as capital expenditures added to the property's basis. For properties held for rental purposes that are vacant, ordinary and necessary expenses, including depreciation, may still be deducted. However, income lost due to vacancy is not deductible.

For cash basis taxpayers, uncollected rent cannot be deducted, as it was never recognized as income. However, under the accrual method, if rent is deemed uncollectible, it may be deductibility classified as a bad business debt. Additionally, if a property is rented but not intended for profit, rental expenses can only be deducted up to the amount of rental income, and losses cannot be carried forward.

If a property transitions to rental use after the start of the tax year, taxpayers must prorate expenses like taxes and insurance between personal and rental use, deducting only the rental portion. When part of a property is rented, expenses must be split accordingly, treating the rental and personal spaces as if they are separate properties. However, expenses unique to the rental portion do not need to be divided.

Self-Rental Rules

In specific situations, income from passive activities must be treated as non-passive income. The self-rental rule applies when property is rented for trade or business use in which the taxpayer materially participates. This rule necessitates that the property is utilized in a business where the taxpayer plays an active role in the operation.

Like-kind Exchange

A Section 1031 exchange, commonly referred to as a like-kind exchange, is a strategic option for real estate investors looking to defer capital gains taxes when selling an investment property.

This approach allows investors to reinvest the proceeds into another qualifying "like-kind" property, thereby postponing the tax liability and enabling continued growth of their investment equity.

Key Requirements

To successfully execute a 1031 exchange, investors must adhere to specific IRS guidelines:

Like-kind property:
The original (relinquished) property and the replacement property must be real estate intended for use in a trade or business, or held as an investment. For instance, exchanging undeveloped land for a commercial building qualifies, but personal residences do not.

Qualified intermediary (QI):
Investors are required to engage a third-party intermediary, known as a QI, to hold the proceeds from the sale and facilitate the exchange. This prevents "constructive receipt" of funds, which could trigger immediate tax implications. Investors are not permitted to serve as their own intermediary.

Strict timelines:

- 45-day identification period: After selling the relinquished property, you have 45 calendar days to identify potential replacement properties in writing.
- 180-day purchase rule: The replacement property must be acquired within 180 days of the relinquished property's sale, or by the tax return due date, whichever comes first.
- Equal or greater value: To achieve full tax deferral, the replacement property must have an equal or greater value than the relinquished property, with all proceeds needing to be reinvested. Any cash or non-like-kind property received, often referred to as "boot," is typically subject to taxation.
- Same taxpayer rule: The title for both the relinquished and replacement properties must be held in the same name, ensuring continuity of ownership.

Benefits:

The primary advantage of engaging in a 1031 exchange is tax deferral, but there are several additional benefits:

1. Increased purchasing power:
   By deferring taxes, investors can reinvest the entire amount of their gains into a new property.

2. Portfolio diversification or consolidation:
Investors have the flexibility to exchange a single property for multiple properties, or vice versa, allowing exploration of different markets or property types.
3. Management relief:
This strategy facilitates a shift from high-maintenance properties to ones that require less active management, such as triple-net lease properties.
4. Estate planning advantages:
Holding the property until passing can result in heirs receiving a "stepped-up" basis on the fair market value, potentially eliminating deferred capital gains taxes altogether.

To report the exchange, it is necessary to use IRS Form 8824, Like-Kind Exchanges, and submit it alongside the tax return for the year in which the exchange took place. Given the complexities of these rules, consulting with a tax professional or real estate attorney is highly advisable.

Schedule F (Form 1040) Overview

Schedule F (Form 1040) is the primary tax form for individual taxpayers, sole proprietors, and single-member LLCs engaged in farming. It is used to report net profit or loss from farming activities and must be filed with your annual individual income tax return (Form 1040 or 1040-SR).

Who Needs to File

Active Farmers:
This includes individuals who cultivate, operate, or manage a farm for profit, whether as an owner or tenant.

Specific Farm Types:
Operators involved in livestock, dairy, poultry, fish farming, as well as those managing fruit farms, truck farms, plantations, ranches, nurseries, orchards, or groves, are required to file.

Material Participants:
Landowners or tenants who actively participate in the operation or management of a farm and receive a share of the production (crop-sharing) must also file.

Key Components of the Form The form is organized into three primary sections, determined by the accounting method used:

Part I (Farm Income - Cash Method):

This section is for reporting income from the sale of livestock, produce, grains, and other agricultural products, as well as agricultural program payments and cooperative distributions.

Part II (Farm Expenses):

Here, taxpayers detail deductible costs associated with farming, which may include:

- Direct Costs: Expenses for seed, fertilizer, feed, chemicals, and pesticides.
- Operational Costs: Costs such as fuel, utilities, insurance, property taxes on land, and wages.
- Capital Costs: Depreciation on equipment, buildings, and breeding livestock.

Part III (Farm Income - Accrual Method):

This part is designed for farmers who recognize income when earned and expenses when incurred, irrespective of cash transactions.

Important Updates for the 2025/2026 Tax Year

---

1. **Standard Mileage Rate:**
   The business standard mileage rate is set to be 70 cents per mile in 2025.
2. **Farmland Sales:**
   In alignment with the "One Big Beautiful Bill Act," taxpayers can choose to pay net income tax from the sale of qualifying farmland to qualified farmers in four annual installments for tax years starting after July 4, 2025.
3. **Section 179 Deduction:**
   The maximum deduction for equipment in 2025 will be $2,500,000, with a phase-out threshold beginning at $4,000,000.
4. **Bonus Depreciation:**
   A 100% special depreciation allowance has been reinstated for qualified property bought after January 19, 2025.

Related Forms and Resources

- Schedule SE (Form 1040): This form is necessary for calculating self-employment tax if the net farm profit is $400 or greater.
- Form 4835: This form is used by landowners receiving crop-share rental income, provided they do not materially participate in farming activities.

This information is vital for farmers to ensure compliance with tax reporting requirements and to take full advantage of available deductions and credits.

Schedule J (Form 1040)

---

is designed for individuals in the farming or fishing industries who wish to average their taxable income over the past three years, commonly referred to as "base years." This election can reduce tax liability in high-income years by applying potentially lower tax rates from earlier years.

Key Details:

- Purpose: The primary goal of Schedule J is to mitigate significant income fluctuations that can occur in farming and fishing businesses. By averaging income, individuals can avoid being pushed into higher tax brackets during peak earning years.
- Who Qualifies: Eligibility is limited to individuals involved in farming or fishing. Corporations and partnerships are not permitted to use this schedule.
- How it Works: The process involves reallocating a portion of the current year's "elected farm income" (EFI) to the three preceding tax years. This allows taxpayers to recalculate their tax obligations using the rates applicable in those years.
- Required Records: To complete this process, individuals will need copies of their tax returns from the three prior

years. For instance, when filing for 2025, the relevant base years would be 2022, 2023, and 2024.

This approach can be a strategic way to manage tax liabilities related to income variability in farming and fishing activities.

Schedule H (Form 1040)

Understanding Schedule H (Form 1040) for Household Employers

Schedule H (Form 1040) is the required form for household employers to report employment taxes when cash wages are paid to household employees, such as nannies, housekeepers, or health aides.

Filing Requirements for the 2026 Tax Year

For the 2026 tax year, employers must file Schedule H if any of the following conditions apply:

- Wage Threshold:
  If you paid any single household employee $3,000 or more in cash wages in 2026.
- Quarterly Wages:
  If total cash wages for all household employees reached $1,000 or more in any calendar quarter in 2025 or 2026.

- Withholding:
  If you withheld federal income tax for any household employee, regardless of the amount withheld.

Taxes Reported on Schedule H

Schedule H is used to calculate and report several federal employment taxes, often referred to as "nanny taxes":

- Social Security & Medicare Taxes: The combined rate is 15.3%, with 7.65% from the employer and 7.65% from the employee.
- Federal Unemployment (FUTA) Tax: The rate is 6% on the first $7,000 of wages, though credits for state unemployment taxes can reduce it to 0.6%.
- Federal Income Tax Withholding: This is required only if the employee requests it and the employer consents.Critical Deadlines and Forms
- Form W-2: Employers must provide Form W-2 to their employees and file it with the Social Security Administration (SSA) by February 2 every year.
- Schedule H Filing: Attach Schedule H to your Tax Return Form 1040 and file it by April 15 annually. If you are not required to file a tax return, file Schedule H independently by the same deadline.
- EIN Requirement: To file Schedule H, you must have an Employer Identification Number (EIN); a Social Security Number is not acceptable. Employers can apply for an EIN through the IRS EIN Assistant.

By understanding these requirements and deadlines, household employers can ensure compliance and efficiently manage their employment tax responsibilities.

Schedule R (Form 1040)

Schedule R (Form 1040) is used to determine the "Credit for the Elderly or the Disabled", a nonrefundable tax credit that helps eligible individuals reduce their tax liability. The credit is available based on specific criteria related to age, disability status, and income limitations.

Eligibility Requirements

To qualify for this credit, individuals must be U.S. citizens or resident aliens and must meet certain income thresholds, alongside one of the following criteria:

- Individuals who are "65 years of age or older" by the end of the tax year.
- Individuals who are "under 65 years of age" at the end of the tax year, have retired due to "permanent and total disability", and receive taxable disability income.

It is important to note that the credit may not be available if your "adjusted gross income (AGI)" or non-taxable Social Security benefits exceed specified limits, which are determined by your filing status.

Filing Instructions

---

1. Determine Eligibility: Review the eligibility criteria to confirm that you meet the age, disability, and income requirements. For detailed guidance, refer to IRS Publication 524.
2. Complete Schedule R: Fill out the form to calculate your potential credit amount, which varies based on your filing status, ranging from $3,750 to $7,500.
3. Transfer to Schedule 3: Report your calculated credit amount on Schedule 3 (Form 1040), line 6d.
4. Attach to Your Return: Submit the completed Schedule R along with your Form 1040 or Form 1040-SR to ensure you receive your credit.

   This information provides a comprehensive overview of the process and requirements for claiming the Credit for the Elderly or the Disabled.

Business Tax

Why do you want to go into business? To make money, of course. But it's also important to think about income tax. If you're self-employed, you need to keep accurate records of your expenses and pay the right amount of tax to the IRS to avoid penalties. To do this well, understanding the Form 1040 guide is crucial. Payments like income and self-employment taxes are reported using Form 1040-ES.

Businesses Leveraging Form 1040 with Schedules

Using Form 1040, businesses can unlock the financial insights required by the IRS, each with specific reporting obligations. Form 1040 is famously used with Schedule C.

1. Sole Proprietorships: This is the most common business type that uses Form 1040. The IRS classifies an activity as a sole proprietorship if it is engaged in consistently for profit and does not operate as a formal corporation or partnership. Earnings or losses are reported on Schedule C (Form 1040).
2. Single-Member Limited Liability Companies (LLCs): By default, the IRS treats single-member LLCs as sole proprietorships for tax purposes. The owner reports income and expenses on Schedule C.
3. Partnerships and S Corporations: Although these entities file their own informational returns (Form 1065 for partnerships and Form 1120-S for S corporations), individual partners or shareholders receive a Schedule K-1 that shows their share of the business's income or loss. This information is reported on Schedule E of Form 1040.
4. Self-Employed Individuals: This category includes freelancers, gig workers, and independent contractors. Those with net earnings of $400 or more must file Schedule C and use Schedule SE (Form 1040) to calculate self-employment tax, including Social Security and Medicare.

5. Rental Real Estate Owners and Royalty Recipients: Income or losses from rental properties or royalties are reported on Schedule E of Form 1040.
6. Farmers: They use Schedule F (Form 1040) to report income and expenses related to farming activities.

Businesses That Do NOT Use Form 1040

Corporations, including both C corporations and S corporations, as well as partnerships, are considered separate legal and tax entities. They file their own tax returns and do not use Form 1040 to report business income.

1. C Corporations: These entities file Form 1120, U.S. Corporation Income Tax Return.
2. S Corporations: These corporations file Form 1120-S, the U.S. Income Tax Return for an S Corporation.
3. Partnerships: Partnerships file an informational return on Form 1065, U.S. Return of Partnership Income.
4. This overview clarifies the different business types and their respective filing requirements for Form 1040 and its schedules.

The purpose of Form 1040 is to report taxable income to the IRS and to claim business expenses on the appropriate forms. The tax rate depends on taxable income: the higher the income, the higher the tax. The amount of taxes owed depends on three main factors, including business expenses, deductions, and credits.

A Basic Income Tax Accounting

1. Gross Income

2. After deducting business expenses, the deduction and credit result in taxable income. Tax liability must be paid before the due date to avoid penalties.

The instructions for completing Form 1040 span over 1000 pages, which can be overwhelming for some people, especially small business owners. To make the process easier, it is recommended to hire professionals such as enrolled agents, accountants, or CPAs to help with tax forms.

Don't overlook Form 1040. It's essential for all individuals and small business owners to pay close attention to this important document. Staying informed about it will help you manage your tax obligations and avoid penalties. Form 1040, also known as the U.S. Individual Income Tax Return, is a two-page form used to report and file income for employees, self-employed individuals, independent contractors, small businesses, and other filers.

Unlocking the Mystery of Schedule K-1: What It Is and Who Needs It

---

Have you ever come across a tax form that left you scratching your head? Enter the Schedule K-1, a key player in tax reporting. But what exactly is it, and who should keep a close eye on it?

In essence, the Schedule K-1 is a federal tax form used to report income, deductions, and credits from partnerships, S corporations, estates, and trusts. It's essential for anyone involved with these entities, as it helps share financial information among stakeholders.

Whether you're a business partner, an S corporation shareholder, or a trust beneficiary, understanding the K-1 is crucial for accurate tax filing. This form can seem complex, but understanding the basics can save you time and headaches come tax season. Dive in and unravel the significance of Schedule K-1 to make your tax experience smoother and more informed.

What Is Schedule K-1?

A Schedule K-1 is a federal tax form used to report income, losses, and dividends for partners in a business or financial entity, as well as for shareholders of an S corporation. It also reports income distributions from trusts and estates to beneficiaries.

1. A separate Schedule K-1 is prepared for each relevant partner in a partnership, as well as for shareholders or

beneficiaries. Partnerships file Form 1065, the partnership tax return, which includes the income and activities reported on each partner's K-1

2. Similarly, an S corporation uses Form 1120-S to report its activities, including those reflected in each shareholder's K-1. Trusts and estates report K-1 activity using Form 1041.

Key Takeaways

Schedule K-1 is a crucial tax document used by business partners, S corporation shareholders, and investors in limited partnerships and certain exchange-traded funds (ETFs) to report income, losses, and dividends. This form is typically issued by pass-through entities—businesses that do not pay corporate income tax on their income but instead transfer the tax liability (along with the majority of their income) to their stakeholders.

It's important for these businesses to meticulously track each participant's basis or ownership stake in the enterprise, as Schedule K-1 provides a detailed account of this information. A variety of income types can be reported on this schedule, and taxpayers should expect to receive their K-1 forms by March 15 or within three months of the entity's fiscal year end.

Understanding Schedule K-1

Under the U.S. federal tax code, a pass-through strategy shifts tax liability from the business entity (such as a trust or partnership) to the individual stakeholders. As a result, the entity does not incur tax on its earnings; rather, each stakeholder receives a share of payouts and reports the associated tax obligations on Schedule K-1, regardless of whether those earnings have been distributed. For partnerships, each partner's K-1 information is submitted to the IRS via Form 1065, and partnership income is reported alongside other income sources on the individual's Form 1040.

Important Considerations

Schedule K-1 shares similarities with Form 1099, as both forms report dividends, interest, and other annual returns. The type of document received—K-1 or 1099—depends on the type of investment. Investments such as master limited partnerships (MLPs), real estate limited partnerships (RELPs), and certain ETFs typically issue K-1 forms.

Aspects of Schedule K-1

Factoring in Partnership Agreements

A partnership is a contractual agreement between two or more individuals, governed by a partnership agreement. Within this structure, at least one general partner (GP) manages the partnership's operations. General partners are personally liable for their own actions and those of fellow general partners, while limited partners' liability is limited to the amount of their investment. The partnership agreement plays a key role in determining profit distribution, which directly affects the details reported on Schedule K-1.

Basis Calculation

Schedule K-1 requires systematic tracking of each partner's basis, which represents their investment or ownership interest in the partnership. The basis can increase with additional contributions and income sharing, and it decreases with losses and withdrawals. For instance, if a partner contributes $40,000 in cash and $20,000 in equipment, earning $5,000 in income, their total basis would be $65,000, adjusted for any withdrawals. If a partner's basis reaches zero, any further payments may be taxed as ordinary income. This basis information is recorded in the capital account section of Schedule K-1.

Income Reporting

Partners may receive various forms of income, including rental income from real estate, bond interest, and dividends. Partnerships often provide guaranteed payments to active general partners, which are also reported on Schedule K-1. Additionally, partnerships may generate income from royalties and capital gains or losses, which are allocated in accordance with the partnership agreement. It is advisable for partners to consult a tax professional, particularly if they anticipate that K-1 income could trigger the alternative minimum tax.

Understanding Schedule K-1 Forms

Schedule K-1 forms are essential tax documents that vary slightly by entity type—partnerships, S-corporations, and trusts—but they all serve the same goal: to report income, losses, deductions, and credits to the IRS and relevant stakeholders.

K-1 for Partnerships

This form is sent to the IRS along with Form 1065 and is provided to each partner for their individual tax returns.

K-1 for S-Corporations

Attached to Form 1120-S, this K-1 details each shareholder's share of income, losses, and credits.

K-1 for Trusts and Estates

When Form 1041 is filed, beneficiaries receive a K-1 to report their share of income.

Important Note:

If you notice an error on your K-1, it's crucial to request a correction from the issuer and then send the corrected copy to the IRS.

Who is Required to File a Schedule K-1?

Entities that must file a K-1 include:

1. **Business partnerships**
    - LLCs with two or more partners or those elected as corporations
2. **S corporations**
3. **Trust and Estates**

Typically, individuals do not file K-1 forms directly but use the information to prepare their personal tax returns, Form 1040. For instance, partners use K-1 data for their tax filings and usually attach the K-1 only if directed to do so. Shareholders and beneficiaries follow similar procedures when reporting their income.

IRS Schedule K-1 is an annual tax form that reports gains, losses, interest, dividends, and distributions from specific entities for the prior tax year. It primarily pertains to pass-through entities that do not pay corporate tax, allowing participants to calculate their income and taxes using the K-1 figures.

Who Receives an IRS Schedule K-1?

Potential recipients of Schedule K-1 include:

Shareholders of S corporations

- Partners in LLCs and partnerships
- Investors in limited partnerships (LPs) and master limited partnerships (MLPs)
- Exchange-traded fund (ETF) investors
- Beneficiaries of trusts or estates

Is IRS Schedule K-1 Income Considered Earned Income?

This classification depends on the recipient's role. For beneficiaries, limited partners, or passive investors, the income is generally treated as unearned. Conversely, for active owners or general partners, it may be treated as earned income, which could be subject to self-employment tax.

When Should You Expect to Receive Your IRS Schedule K-1?

K-1 forms can often be delayed. They are typically due by March 15 or within three months of the fiscal year-end. Recipients should expect to receive their K-1 by that date or shortly thereafter.

A Schedule K-1 is a federal form issued by pass-through entities that details each stakeholder's share of income, losses, and gains. Recipients use this information for their own tax returns:

- For individuals, it functions similarly to the income tax form used by W-2 employees.
- Small businesses use it to file business taxes. Self-employed individuals, sole proprietors, or partnership members report income and expenses using Form 1040. Business income is reported alongside personal income tax returns on Schedule C.

For entities structured as S corporations, partnerships, or LLCs treated as corporations, it is necessary to complete Form 1120S in conjunction with Form 1040.

Key Forms for Small Businesses

- Form 1040-ES: This form allows taxpayers to pay estimated taxes for the current year based on the previous year's tax liability. Taxpayers responsible for income, self-employment, or other taxes should use Form 1040-ES.

By understanding the different types of Schedule K-1 forms and how they fit into the tax reporting framework, individuals and businesses can better navigate their tax obligations.

Tax Return

In the U.S., a taxpayer for income tax purposes is any individual or entity required to file a tax return and pay taxes to the Internal Revenue Service (IRS). This typically includes those with income exceeding the standard deduction and exempt income.

Individuals Required to File a Return:
Generally, a person must file a tax return if their gross income exceeds a certain threshold, which varies by filing status, age, and dependency status.

Taxpayers fall into two primary groups:
individuals and entities. Each group plays a distinct role in the tax landscape, shaping how we contribute to the government. Understanding these differences can help us navigate the complexities of taxation more effectively.

Individuals:

1. U.S. Citizens and Resident Aliens:
   These individuals are subject to U.S. tax on their worldwide income, regardless of where they live or the source of their income, and they file a 1040.
2. Non-Resident Aliens: These individuals are taxed primarily on income that is effectively connected with a U.S. trade or business, as well as on certain U.S.-source investment income, and they file 1040NR.

For non-U.S. citizens, tax residency is determined by either holding a Green Card or meeting the Substantial Presence Test. The test generally requires being physically present in the U.S. for a total of 183 days over a three-year period.

To meet the Substantial Presence Test, you must be physically present in the U.S. for:

1. At least 31 days during the current year, and
2. A total of 183 days over the past three years, calculated using a weighted average:
3. 100% of the days of physical presence in the current calendar year.
   - 1/3 of the days you were present in the first preceding year.
   - 1/6 of the days you were present in the second preceding year.

If the sum of these calculated days is 183 or more, you generally meet the test and are considered a U.S. tax resident.

Important Exceptions

Certain individuals and types of days do not count toward the Substantial Presence Test calculation:

- Exempt individuals include specific foreign government-related individuals, teachers, trainees, and students on certain visas (such as F-1 and J-1).
- Days when you were unable to leave the U.S. due to a medical condition that developed while you were in the U.S.
- Days spent in transit between two foreign points (if you were in the U.S. for less than 24 hours).

- Days when you commuted daily to work in the U.S. from Canada or Mexico.

You may also claim the "closer connection exception" if you are present in the U.S. for fewer than 183 days in the current year, have a tax home in a foreign country, and maintain a closer connection to that country than to the U.S.

Taxpayers must use identification numbers when filing with the IRS.

Social Security Number (SSN):
Issued to U.S. citizens and eligible residents.

Individual Taxpayer Identification Number (ITIN):
Issued to individuals who need a U.S. taxpayer identification number but are ineligible for an SSN.

Filing Statuses

The Internal Revenue Service (IRS) identifies five primary tax filing statuses for Form 1040 that individuals can choose from when preparing their tax returns. The filing status is generally based on your marital status as of the last day of the year and plays a significant role in calculating your tax obligation, determining your standard deduction, and assessing eligibility for various tax credits.

The five tax filing statuses include:

1. **Single:**
   This status applies to taxpayers who are unmarried, divorced, or legally separated under a divorce or separate maintenance decree and who do not qualify for any other filing status.

2. **Married Filing Jointly (MFJ):**
   Married couples may file a joint return, combining their income and deductions. In most cases, this approach results in lower tax liability and a higher standard deduction. Both spouses are responsible for the tax due, as well as any associated interest or penalties.

3. **Married Filing Separately (MFS):**
   Couples may elect to file separate tax returns, which can be advantageous in certain financial or legal circumstances or if one spouse prefers to be solely responsible for their own tax obligations. If one spouse files a separate tax return and chooses to itemize deductions, the other spouse must also itemize.

4. **Head of Household (HoH):**
   This filing status applies to unmarried individuals who pay more than half the expenses of maintaining a home for themselves and a qualifying individual who has lived with them for more than half the year. Notably, a dependent parent is not required to reside with you. This status offers more favorable tax rates and a larger standard deduction than the Single and MFS statuses.

5. **Qualifying Surviving Spouse (QSS):**

This status may be available for up to two years after the year your spouse passed away, provided you have a dependent child and meet additional requirements. Using this status allows you to benefit from the more favorable tax rates and the highest standard deduction available to married couples filing jointly.

Understanding these different filing statuses is crucial for optimizing your tax situation and ensuring compliance with IRS regulations.

Understanding Head of Household Filing Status and Dependent Claims

---

Head of Household Requirements

To qualify for the Head of Household (HOH) filing status, a taxpayer must meet the following criteria:

- Filing Status: The taxpayer must be unmarried or "considered unmarried" as of the last day of the tax year.
- Financial Support: The taxpayer must have contributed more than half of the costs associated with maintaining the household throughout the year.
- Qualifying Dependents: The taxpayer should maintain a household for either: A qualifying child or any other relative who qualifies as a dependent for more than six months, or A parent for the entire year, provided the

parent can be claimed as a dependent on the taxpayer's return.

Married but Considered Unmarried for Tax Purposes

A married individual may be considered unmarried for tax purposes if they fulfill the following conditions:

1. Separate Filing: The person files a separate tax return from their spouse.
2. Housing Costs: They must have provided more than half of the costs of maintaining their home during the tax year.
3. Principal Residence: The home must serve as the primary residence for the taxpayer and a dependent (such as a child or eligible foster child) for more than half of the tax year. This includes situations where a child qualifies as a dependent but the exemption is granted to the noncustodial spouse under specific conditions (like a divorce decree).
4. Living Arrangements: The spouse should not have lived in the home at any time during the last six months of the tax year.

Tiebreaker Rules for Qualifying Children

In the case of disputes over who may claim a child as a qualifying dependent, the following tiebreaker rules apply:

1. If both parents file a joint return, the child is treated as a qualifying child by those parents.
2. If only one individual is the child's parent, that parent has the claim.
3. Among two parents who do not file jointly, the parent with whom the child lived for the majority of nights during the tax year claims the child.
4. If the child lived with both parents for the same duration, the parent with the higher Adjusted Gross Income (AGI) is entitled to the claim.
5. If no parent can claim the child, the individual with the highest AGI that exceeds that of the parents may claim the child.
6. If another person claims the taxpayer's qualifying child for the Earned Income Credit (EIC) and uses the tiebreaker rules, the taxpayer may still claim the EIC if they have another qualifying child or meet the EIC requirements without a qualifying child.

Important Update for 2025

Starting in 2025, taxpayers who possess an Identity Protection PIN (IP PIN) will be allowed to e-file and claim a dependent, even if that dependent has already been claimed on another taxpayer's return. In such cases, the IRS will utilize the tiebreaker rules to determine who can rightfully claim the dependent.

Dependents

Be under age 19 or, if a full-time student, under age 24, or any age if permanently and totally disabled. Residency: Live with you for more than half the year, with some exceptions. Support: They receive more than half of their financial support from you.

Understanding Eligibility for Dependents on Your Tax Return

When determining whether a person qualifies as a dependent on your tax return, it is important to understand a few key criteria. A dependent must meet requirements related to their relationship with you, living situation, and financial status.

What Qualifies Someone as a Dependent?

The IRS outlines two primary categories of dependents: qualifying children and qualifying relatives. Each category has its own specific criteria.

General Requirements:

To qualify as a dependent, an individual must:

- Be related to you by blood, marriage, common-law partnership, or adoption (e.g., a child, parent, sibling, or grandparent).

- Live with you in a shared household for part or all of the tax year.
- Be financially dependent on you for their basic needs, such as food, shelter, or clothing.

Types of Dependents

(A) Qualifying Child:

To claim a qualifying child as a dependent, you must assess the following:

- Relationship: The child must be your son, daughter, stepchild, eligible foster child, or a sibling (including half- and step-siblings).
- Age Requirement: The child must be under 19, or under 24 if they are a full-time student. There is no age limit if the child is permanently and totally disabled.
- Living Situation: The child must reside with you for more than half of the year, although there are exceptions to this rule.
- Support: The child may earn income but cannot provide more than half of their own financial support.

(B) Qualifying Relative:

To qualify as a relative, the following criteria apply:

- Living Arrangement: The relative must live with you for the entire year, or be listed among the relatives who do not need to live with you, as specified in IRS Publication 501.

- Income Limit: In 2025, the relative's gross income must not exceed $5,200 (annually inflation-adjusted). Certain types of income, such as specific Social Security benefits, may be excluded from this total.
- Financial Support: You must provide more than half of the total support for the relative during the year.

Additional Considerations

To claim someone as a dependent, it is also crucial to ensure that you are not claimed as a dependent on someone else's tax return. This ensures that all qualifications are met for the individual you wish to claim.

Understanding these criteria can help you navigate the complexities of tax filings correctly and ensure compliance with IRS regulations.

ITIN Dependent

An individual taxpayer identification number (ITIN) holder is eligible to claim dependents on their federal tax return, provided the dependent meets all IRS criteria for a qualifying child or qualifying relative. However, the specific tax benefits available to the ITIN holder depend on the dependent's taxpayer identification number (TIN) and other factors.

Dependent Tax Benefits for ITIN Holders

1. **Credit for Other Dependents (ODC):**
   ITIN holders can claim the nonrefundable $500 Credit for Other Dependents for a qualifying individual such as a child over 17, an elderly parent, or a U.S. resident alien child with an ITIN, assuming all dependency rules are satisfied. The dependent must be a U.S. citizen, U.S. national, or U.S. resident alien.
2. **Child Tax Credit (CTC):**
   To qualify for the Child Tax Credit, the dependent child must possess a valid Social Security Number (SSN) that is authorized for employment in the U.S. by the due date of the tax return (including extensions). A child who only has an ITIN does not qualify for the CTC or the additional child tax credit (ACTC).
3. **Child and Dependent Care Credit:**
   ITIN holders may be eligible for this credit if they incurred expenses for the care of a qualifying individual (who has the necessary TIN) to enable them to work or look for work.
4. **American Opportunity Tax Credit (AOTC):**
   This education credit may be available for qualified expenses related to an eligible student who is a dependent.

General Requirements to Claim a Dependent Regardless of an individual's ITIN status, the person being claimed as a dependent must fulfill all general dependency criteria, including:

- **Citizen or Resident Test:** The individual must be a U.S. citizen, U.S. national, U.S. resident alien, or a resident of Canada or Mexico.
- **Joint Return Test:** The individual cannot file a joint tax return for the year, unless solely to claim a refund of withheld taxes.
- **Dependent Taxpayer Test:** The individual cannot be claimed as a dependent on another person's tax return.

For comprehensive information on these rules, refer to IRS Publication 501, which covers dependents, the standard deduction, and filing information, or consult the official IRS website for additional guidance.

Employees

An employee is an individual who is compensated for performing work for a person or company. They do not need to work full-time to qualify as an employee; the key requirement is that they receive payment from an employer, which is the entity providing their wages. Typically, employees receive their Form W-2, Wage and Tax Statement, by January 31 of the year following the calendar year in which they earned their wages. This form details an employee's total earnings and the taxes that were withheld. If an employee does not receive their W-2, it is advisable for them to reach out to their employer for clarification.

In the United States, employees are entitled to certain mandated benefits, including Social Security and Medicare, collectively known as FICA. These federal programs provide support for retirement, disability, and healthcare for senior citizens. Additionally, unemployment insurance offers temporary financial assistance to workers who lose their jobs through no fault of their own and is administered at the state level. Any unemployment compensation received is taxable and must be reported on federal income tax returns. The state agency that provides these benefits will send Form 1099-G, Certain Government Payments, by the end of January the following year, indicating the total amount of benefits received.

Workers' compensation, another crucial benefit, is a state-level program that covers medical expenses and lost wages due to job-related injuries or illnesses, subject to specific state regulations. Alongside these mandatory benefits, employees may also access optional perks, such as health, dental, and vision insurance; retirement plans like 401(k); paid time off (including vacation, sick days, holidays, and parental leave); and wellness programs. All are reported on W-2, not 1099-G.

Mandatory Benefits:

These benefits are required by federal or state law:

- Social Security & Medicare (FICA): Federal programs for retirement, disability, and healthcare for seniors.
- Workers' Compensation: Provides coverage for medical costs and lost wages resulting from job-related injuries or illnesses, depending on state-specific rules.
- Unemployment Insurance: Offers temporary financial support for individuals who lose their jobs without any fault of their own, administered by state agencies.
- Family & Medical Leave Act (FMLA): Provides unpaid, job-protected leave for designated family or medical reasons, applicable to employers with 50 or more employees.
- Health Insurance (ACA): The Affordable Care Act mandates that employers with 50 or more full-time employees must offer affordable health insurance or face penalties.

Common Voluntary Benefits:

- These benefits vary by company and are designed to attract and retain employees:
- Health-Related: This includes medical, dental, and vision insurance, as well as Flexible Spending Accounts (FSAs) and Health Savings Accounts (HSAs).
- Retirement: Options include 401(k) plans, pensions, and employer matching contributions.
- Paid Time Off (PTO): Benefits include vacation days, sick leave, personal days, paid holidays, and paid parental leave.
- Insurance: Options may include life insurance, as well as short-term and long-term disability insurance.
- Wellness & Perks: Programs may include gym memberships, wellness initiatives, mental health support, commuter benefits, childcare assistance, and tuition reimbursement.
- Flexible Work: Many organizations offer flexible scheduling and remote work options to accommodate employees' needs.

Form W-2 Box 12 codes

U.S. taxpayers typically receive a W-2 form from their employers each year, which outlines important details about their earnings and tax withholdings. One area of the W-2 that often causes confusion is Box 12, which contains codes that convey specific information about a taxpayer's financial situation.

This guide explains what Box 12 on a W-2 represents and summarizes relevant information from the instructions. Understanding Box 12 is crucial for accurately calculating your income tax, which incorporates wages from various sources, including regular pay, state wages, Medicare wages, and Social Security wages.

To begin, it's essential to understand the purpose of the W-2 form. This form is a critical document issued by the Internal Revenue Service (IRS) that reports the amount of money withheld from your taxable wages, including federal, state, and local taxes.

The details in Box 12 can raise many questions. This box includes 30 subcategories, labeled A to II, and uses a combination of single- and double-letter codes. These codes are instrumental in providing the IRS with additional context for taxable income.

The information in Box 12 helps determine the nature of various amounts reported, though it's important to note that any gross income included in W-2 Box 1 is already accounted for. Box 12 also reveals critical details such as earnings, contributions to retirement plans, employer contributions to health insurance, and benefits like group-term life insurance contributions. Understanding these codes can help taxpayers navigate their financial records and fulfill their tax obligations more effectively.

Code Description

- **A:** Uncollected Social Security tax or Railroad Retirement Tax Act (RRTA) tax on tips. Include this tax on Form 1040 Schedule 2, line 13.
- **B:** Uncollected Medicare tax on tips. Include this tax on Form 1040 Schedule 2, line 13.
- **C:** Taxable costs of group-term life insurance over $50,000 (included in W-2 Boxes 1, 3 (up to the Social Security wage base), and 5); taxable costs are informational only.
- **D:** Elective deferral under a Section 401(k) cash or deferred arrangement plan. This includes a SIMPLE 401(k) arrangement. You may be able to claim the Saver's Credit on Form 1040 Schedule 3, line 4. See Form 1040 Instructions for details.
- **E:** Elective deferrals under a Section 403(b) salary reduction agreement. You may be able to claim the Saver's Credit on Form 1040 Schedule 3, line 4. See Form 1040 Instructions for details.
- **F:** Elective deferrals under a Section 408(k)(6) salary reduction SEP. You may be able to claim the Saver's Credit on Form 1040 Schedule 3, line 4. See Form 1040 Instructions for details.

- **G:** Elective deferrals and employer contributions (including non-elective deferrals) to a Section 457(b) deferred compensation plan. You may be able to claim the Saver's Credit on Form 1040 Schedule 3, line 4. See Form 1040 Instructions for details.

- **H:** Elective deferrals to a Section 501(c)(18)(D) tax-exempt organization plan. You may be able to claim the Saver's Credit on Form 1040 Schedule 3, line 4. See Form 1040 Instructions for details.
- **J:** Nontaxable sick pay (information only, not included in W-2 Boxes 1, 3, or 5).
- **K:** 20% excise tax on excess golden parachute payments. Include this tax on Form 1040 Schedule 2, line 17k, and enter the total amount of the tax.
- **L:** Substantiated employee business expense reimbursements (nontaxable). You may need to file Form 2106, Employee Business Expenses. This amount is reported on that form on line 7. See Form 2106 Instructions for details.
- **M:** Uncollected Social Security tax or RRTA tax on the taxable cost of group-term life insurance over $50,000 (former employees only). Include this tax on Form 1040 Schedule 2, line 13, identified as "UT."
- **N:** Uncollected Medicare tax on the taxable cost of group-term life insurance over $50,000 (former employees only). Include Medicare wage tax on Form 1040 Schedule 2, line 13.
- **P:** Excludable moving expense reimbursements paid directly to a member of the U.S. Armed Forces (not

included in Boxes 1, 3, or 5). Use Form 3903, Moving Expenses, to figure your moving expense deduction and report on Form 1040 Schedule 1, line 14, if you qualify.

- **Q:** For military personnel. See the instructions for Form 1040 or Form 1040-SR for details on reporting this amount.
- **R:** Any employer contributions to your Archer medical savings account (MSA). Report on Form 8853, Archer MSAs and Long-Term Care Insurance Contracts, line 1.
- **S:** Employee salary reduction contributions under a Section 408(p) SIMPLE (not included in Box 1). You may be able to claim the Saver's Credit on Form 1040 Schedule 3, line 4. See Form 1040 Instructions for details.
- **T:** Adoption benefits (not included in Box 1). Complete Form 8839, Qualified Adoption Expenses, to compute any excludable amounts.
- **V:** Income from the exercise of non-statutory (not included in Boxes 1, 3 (up to the Social Security wage base), and 5). See Publication 525, Taxable and Nontaxable Income, for reporting requirements.
- **W:** Employer contributions (including amounts the employee elected to contribute using a Section 125 cafeteria plan) to your (not included in Boxes 1, 3, or 5). Report on Form 8889, Health Savings Accounts (HSAs).
- **Y:** Deferrals under a Section 409A nonqualified deferred compensation plan.
- **Z:** Income under a nonqualified deferred compensation plan that fails to satisfy Section 409A. This amount is also included in Box 1 and is subject to an additional 20% tax

plus interest. See Form 1040 Instructions, Schedule 2, line 17h, Other Taxes, for more information.

- **AA:** Designated Roth contributions under a 401(k) plan. Roth contributions are not deductible; however, you may be able to claim the Saver's Credit on Form 1040 Schedule 3, line 4. See Form 1040 Instructions for details.
- **BB:** Designated Roth contributions under a 403(b) plan. Roth contributions are not deductible; however, you may be able to claim the Saver's Credit on Form 1040 Schedule 3, line 4. See Form 1040 Instructions for details.
- **DD:** Code DD includes the cost of employer-sponsored health coverage (information only).
- **EE:** Designated Roth contributions under a governmental 457(b) plan. This amount doesn't apply to contributions under a tax-exempt organization Section 457(b) plan. Roth contributions are not deductible; however, you may be able to claim the Saver's Credit on Form 1040 Schedule 3, line 4. See Form 1040 Instructions for details.
- **FF:** Permitted benefits under a qualified small employer health insurance reimbursement arrangement (information only).
- **GG:** Income from qualified equity grants under Section 83(i) (information only). This amount is includible in gross income from qualified equity grants under Section 83(i)(1)(A) for the calendar year. This amount is wages for Box 1.
- **HH:** Aggregate deferrals under Section...
- **II:** Medicaid waiver payments excluded from gross income under Notice 2014-7.

Stocks for Employees

Company stock for employees encompasses various forms of equity compensation designed to give employees an ownership stake in the company. This approach is intended to recruit skilled professionals, motivate high performance, and improve employee retention by aligning workforce objectives with the organization's long-term strategic goals. The Company is not legally obligated, as some misunderstand.

Common Types of Employee Stock Plans

Employees typically receive company stock through several common mechanisms, including:

- Employee Stock Options (ESOs): These options provide employees the right to purchase a specified number of company shares at a fixed price (also known as the "exercise price" or "strike price") within a defined time period.
- Incentive Stock Options (ISOs): Exclusively available to employees, ISOs may qualify for favorable tax treatment if specific holding periods are adhered to.
- Non-Qualified Stock Options (NSOs): These can be granted to employees, consultants, and directors. The difference between the market value and the exercise price at the time of exercise is taxed as ordinary income.
- Restricted Stock Units (RSUs): Employees are granted shares (or the right to receive their value in cash or stock)

once certain conditions, typically time-based vesting or performance objectives, are met. Unlike stock options, employees do not have to pay to acquire shares upon vesting; the total value is taxed as ordinary income at that time.

- Employee Stock Purchase Plans (ESPPs): These company-sponsored programs enable employees to buy company stock through after-tax payroll deductions, often at a discount of up to 15%. Certain plans may feature a "look-back" option, applying the discount to the lower stock price either at the beginning or end of the offering period.
- Employee Stock Ownership Plans (ESOPs): ESOPs are qualified retirement plans established as trusts that provide employees with an ownership interest in the company. The company typically contributes shares or cash to the trust with no upfront cost to employees. Shares vest over time and are distributed to employees when they leave the company, often upon retirement.

Key Concepts

- **Grant Date:**
  The date on which the company officially awards stock options or equity to employees.
- **Vesting:**
  The process through which employees earn the rights to their stock or options over time, typically through continued employment or meeting specific performance targets. A common structure involves a four-year vesting

period with a one-year "cliff," meaning employees receive no shares if they leave before one year, but accrue shares over the remaining period.

Exercise: The act of purchasing shares at the pre-set strike price (applicable only to stock options).

- **Tax Implications:**
  Taxation varies significantly depending on the type of plan and jurisdiction. Employees should consult plan documents and financial advisors to fully understand their potential tax liabilities, especially regarding capital gains and ordinary income taxes.

For More Information

The specific details of various plans are outlined in an employee's formal stock option agreement or plan documents provided by the employer. Resources for further information include the IRS, the National Center for Employee Ownership (NCEO), and financial institutions managing these accounts, such as Fidelity and Morgan Stanley at Work.

Tax Implications

Tax consequences for employee stock plans can vary widely depending on the plan type (e.g., RSUs, stock options, ESPPs) and the timing of events such as grants, vesting, exercise, and sale. Generally, there are two types of tax obligations: ordinary income tax (applied when stock value is received or becomes vested) and capital gains tax (applied when stock is sold for a profit).

- Restricted Stock Units (RSUs):
- At Grant: No initial tax liability.
- At Vesting/Payout: The fair market value (FMV) of the shares at vesting is treated as ordinary income and is subject to income and payroll taxes (e.g., Social Security and Medicare). Employers typically withhold a portion to cover these taxes and report the income on the employee's Form W-2.
    - At Sale: The difference between the sale price and the FMV at vesting (the cost basis) is classified as a capital gain or loss.
    - Short-term: If shares are held for one year or less post-vesting, the gain is taxed at the higher ordinary income tax rate.
    - Long-term: If held for over a year, the gain is taxed at lower, preferential capital gains rates.

Stock Options:

There are two primary types of stock options: Non-Qualified Stock Options (NSOs) and Incentive Stock Options (ISOs). Understanding these distinctions can be crucial for effective planning and maximizing the benefits of equity compensation.

Understanding Retirement

The obligation to file a tax return depends primarily on gross income, filing status, and age. The Internal Revenue Service (IRS) does not provide a specific number of retirees who file; instead, the requirement hinges on various income thresholds. According to estimates from the Social Security Administration, approximately half of Social Security recipients are subject to income taxes on their benefits, indicating that many retirees have other sources of income that require them to file a tax return.

When Retirees Must File a Tax Return

Retirees must file a federal income tax return if their gross income meets or exceeds the applicable minimum filing threshold for their situation. Gross income includes wages, interest, dividends, capital gains, pensions, annuities, and the taxable portion of Social Security benefits.

For the 2025 tax year, the general gross income thresholds for seniors aged 65 or older by year-end are as follows:

- Single: $17,550 or more
- Head of Household: $25,625 or more
- Married Filing Jointly: $34,700 or more (this applies if both spouses are 65 or older; different thresholds apply if only one spouse meets this age requirement)
- Married Filing Separately: $5 or more (if you lived with your spouse at any time during the year)

How Social Security Benefits Affect Filing

If Social Security benefits are your sole source of income, they are generally not taxable, and you will likely not need to file a return. However, you will receive Form SSA-1099, Social Security Benefit Statement. If you have other sources of income, a portion of your Social Security benefits may become taxable, which could push your income above the filing threshold.

To determine whether your benefits are taxable, the IRS calculates "combined income," which includes your adjusted gross income, nontaxable interest, and one-half of your Social Security benefits.

- Up to 50% of benefits may be taxable if your combined income is between $25,000 and $34,000 for single filers or between $32,000 and $44,000 for married couples filing jointly.
- Up to 85% of benefits may be taxable if your combined income exceeds $34,000 for single filers or $44,000 for married couples filing jointly.

Even if you are not required to file based on your income, it may still be beneficial to file a return. By doing so, you could claim refundable tax credits or receive a refund for any federal income tax withheld from your payments.

Retirement is a major life transition during which individuals move away from the workforce and typically rely on a combination of government benefits, employer-sponsored plans, and personal savings. Most retirees will receive both 1099-R and SSN-1099 forms as part of their retirement income documentation.

Retirement Ages in the U.S.

- The choice of retirement age can significantly affect the government benefits one receives:
- Early Retirement (Age 62): This is the earliest age at which individuals can start claiming Social Security benefits, but benefits can be reduced by as much as 30%.
- Full Retirement Age (FRA): The FRA varies by birth year, ranging from 66 to 67. For those born in 1960 or later, the FRA is 67.
- Delayed Retirement (Up to Age 70): Individuals who wait until age 70 to claim benefits can maximize their monthly Social Security payments by accumulating delayed retirement credits.
- Medicare Eligibility: Regardless of when Social Security is claimed, Medicare coverage generally begins at age 65.

Savings and Contribution Limits

It's essential to keep an eye on savings and contribution limits because they adjust with inflation. Checking them annually can help you maximize your savings potential! Stay informed and make your money work harder for you!

For the 2026 tax year, the IRS has set the following contribution limits:

- 401(k) / 403(b) / 457 Plans: The maximum contribution is $ 24 500.
- Catch-up Contributions (Age 50 +): An additional $ 8, 000 can be contributed.

- Super- Catch-up Contributions (Ages 60–63): A special limit allows contributions up to $ 11 250.
- IRA (Traditional/Roth): The contribution limit is $ 7 500.
- Catch-up Contributions (Age 50 +): An additional $ 1, 100 is permitted.

Common Retirement Strategies

A. Financial experts suggest the following guidelines to estimate retirement needs and plan accordingly:

B. 80% Income Replacement: Aim to replace approximately 80% of pre-retirement annual income to sustain your current lifestyle.

C. The 4% Rule: The strategy involves withdrawing 4% of total savings in the first year of retirement (with adjustments for inflation each subsequent year) to ensure funds last for about 30 years.

D. The 25 x Rule: It is recommended to save 25 times one's anticipated annual expenses to achieve a reliable retirement goal.

E. The $ 1 000 Rule: People should aim for $ 240,000 in savings for every $ 1 000 of monthly income they desire in retirement.

Types of Retirement Plans

There are various retirement plan structures to consider:

- Defined Benefit (Pension): This type guarantees a specified monthly benefit based on an individual's salary and years of service.

- Defined Contribution (401(k)/IRA): Benefits from these plans depend on contributions from employees and employers, as well as the performance of investments.
- Phased Retirement: This option allows employees to gradually transition into retirement by working part-time while beginning to draw benefits.

  Understanding these aspects of retirement can help individuals better prepare for this important life stage.

From 1099-R

Form 1099-R, titled "Distributions from Pensions, Annuities, Retirement or Profit-Sharing Plans, IRAs, Insurance Contracts, etc.," is an IRS information return used to report withdrawals or distributions of $10 or more from retirement and pension accounts. If you received distributions from a pension, annuity, 401(k), 403(b), traditional IRA, Roth IRA, or a similar retirement savings plan, you will receive a Form 1099-R. Payers are generally required to send this form to recipients by January 31 of the year following the distribution.

Taxability

Whether a distribution is taxable depends on the type of plan and whether you made pre-tax or after-tax contributions.

- **Traditional Accounts:** Distributions from traditional IRAs or 401(k)s (where contributions were made with pre-tax dollars) are generally fully taxable as ordinary income.
- **Roth Accounts:** Qualified distributions from a Roth IRA or Roth 401(k) (where contributions were made with after-tax dollars) are typically tax-free.

The most important boxes on the form for taxpayers typically include:

- **Box 1 (Gross Distribution):** This is the total amount of money distributed during the year.
- **Box 2a (Taxable Amount):** This shows the portion of the gross distribution that is subject to income tax. It may be left blank if the payer cannot determine the taxable amount (e.g., with certain IRAs or after-tax contributions).
- **Box 4 (Federal Income Tax Withheld):** This indicates any federal income tax that was withheld from the payment.
- **Box 5 (Employee Contributions/Designated Roth Basis):** This is the amount of your investment in the contract (after-tax contributions) that can be recovered tax-free.
- **Box 7 (Distribution Code):** This one- or two-character code informs the IRS about the type of distribution (e.g., normal retirement, early withdrawal, disability, direct rollover) and whether it may be subject to additional penalties.

Distribution Codes for Box 7

Box 7 of IRS Form 1099-R uses alphanumeric codes to identify the type of distribution from a retirement plan, annuity, or insurance contract, which affects its taxability and any potential penalties. Common distribution codes include:

- **Code1:** Early distribution without a known exception, potentially subject to a 10% penalty and regular income tax.

- **Code 2:** Early distribution with an exception (e.g., disability, IRS levy, substantially equal periodic payments).

- **Code 3:** Disability distribution.

- **Code 4:** Death benefit payments to a beneficiary.

- **Code 7:** Normal distribution for individuals aged 59½ or older, typically for retirees.

- **Code G:** Direct rollover to another qualified plan or IRA, usually non-taxable.

- **Code J:** Early distribution from a Roth IRA without a known exception.

- **Code Q:** Qualified distribution from a Roth IRA meeting specific criteria (5-year holding period, and the recipient is age 59½ or older, disabled, or deceased).

- **Code T:** Roth IRA distribution with an exception, but the payer is unsure if the 5-year holding period has been met.

- **Code Y:** Qualified Charitable Distribution (QCD) from an IRA to a charity.

  If you have questions about the code on your form, contact the plan administrator or payer who issued it, as they are responsible for accurate reporting. For detailed guidance, refer to the IRS Instructions for Forms 1099-R and 5498.

Understanding IRAs, Retirement Plans, Pensions, and Annuities: Mandatory Distributions

---

Retirement plans are designed to provide financial security during retirement, but there are specific rules regarding how long funds can remain in these accounts. One important rule is that individuals must begin taking withdrawals from their tax-deferred retirement plans at a certain age. These withdrawals are known as Required Minimum Distributions (RMDs). The RMD is the minimum amount a taxpayer must withdraw from their retirement account each year, calculated by dividing the account balance as of December 31 of the preceding year by the applicable life expectancy or distribution period.

The RMD rules generally apply to a wide range of retirement plans, including employer-sponsored plans (like 401(k) and

403(b) plans), non-employer-sponsored plans, as well as various types of IRAs, such as traditional IRAs, SIMPLE IRAs, and SEP IRAs. Once individuals reach the required minimum distribution age, currently set at 73, they must start making annual withdrawals. However, the first RMD can be deferred to April 1 of the year following the year in which they reach this age, known as the required beginning date. For subsequent years, RMDs must be withdrawn by December 31. Notably, for 401(k) or similar plans, if the plan allows, the initial RMD may also be delayed until April 1 of the year the participant retires.

It is important to note that Roth retirement plans are exempt from RMD rules, allowing funds to remain in the account until the owner passes away, with no mandatory withdrawals at a specific age.

Excise Tax on Excess Accumulation in Retirement Plans

The purpose of RMD rules is to ensure that retirement funds are not left untouched indefinitely. Failing to take the required RMD can result in a significant penalty; taxpayers may incur a 25% excise tax on the amount not withdrawn. However, there is a provision for a reduced excise tax rate of 10% if the taxpayer corrects the shortfall by taking the necessary distribution within a designated period, known as the "correction window." This window begins when the excise tax is imposed and ends on one of the following dates:

- The date the deficiency notice regarding the tax is mailed.
- The date the tax is formally assessed.

- The last day of the second taxable year after the taxable year in which the excise tax was imposed.
- This understanding of RMDs and the potential penalties associated with them is essential for effective retirement planning.

Other 1040

Form 1040-SR:

Form 1040-SR is a streamlined version of the standard Form 1040, specifically designed to cater to the needs of senior taxpayers aged 65 and older. While both forms can be utilized by taxpayers whether or not they itemize deductions, Form 1040-SR offers features aimed at enhancing clarity and user-friendliness. Notably, it includes larger print and a chart to help with deduction calculations. Importantly, individuals do not need to be retired to use this form; those still in the workforce at age 65 or older can file using Form 1040-SR without any income restrictions.

Form 1040-NR:

Form 1040-NR serves a distinct purpose compared to Form 1040. It is intended for non-resident aliens who must report only their U.S. income, while Form 1040 caters to U.S. residents, resident aliens, and citizens reporting their worldwide income. When completing the 1040-NR, taxpayers should only include income earned within the United States during the current tax year, which spans January 1 to December 31. It is essential to remember that not all individuals residing in the U.S. are American-born or naturalized citizens; those who legally reside in the country and meet the substantial presence test may also be subject to U.S. taxation.

Form 1040X:

In cases where errors are found in a filed Form 1040, taxpayers must use Form 1040X to amend their tax return. This form is necessary for making amendments and is distinct from the original form. It's important to note that Form 1040X should not be used for basic math errors; rather, it is intended for more substantial corrections or adjustments. Taxpayers, including those who are married, can opt to file jointly or separately when using this form. Additionally, those who need to address IRS corrections or who wish to claim losses or unused credits must file Form 1040X to amend their tax filings properly.

Entities (Businesses)

Various business structures and organizations are also considered taxpayers and must file returns, including:

Sole Proprietors

A sole proprietorship is the simplest business structure, owned and operated by one person. There is no legal distinction between the owner and the business, meaning the owner receives all profits but also faces unlimited personal liability for all debts and obligations. This makes it easy to start but also poses a risk to personal assets.

As an unincorporated business, sole proprietorships are common among freelancers, consultants, and small business owners. They require minimal setup and are taxed as personal income. One individual controls and manages the entire operation, and in the eyes of the law and tax authorities, the owner is the business.

The owner's personal assets, such as their home and savings, can be used to cover business debts. Typically, there is no formal registration required beyond the business activity, making it straightforward to establish. The owner retains all profits but is responsible for paying personal income tax—often reported using Schedule C—as well as self-employment taxes, which support Social Security and Medicare.

A sole proprietorship may also be referred to as a sole trader, proprietor, or individual entrepreneurship. Remember that using Schedule C is necessary for tax purposes.

Partnerships

The purpose of a partnership, for IRS (Internal Revenue Service) purposes, is to function as a pass-through entity for taxation. This means that the partnership itself does not pay federal income tax. Instead, profits, losses, deductions, and credits are "passed through" to the individual partners, who report their share on their personal tax returns.

The primary requirement for partnerships is to file an annual information return, Form 1065, U.S. Return of Partnership Income. This form reports the partnership's overall financial activity to the IRS, but it is only for informational purposes. This pass-through structure allows partnerships to avoid the "double taxation" that C corporations face, where income is taxed at both the corporate level and again when distributed to shareholders as dividends.

The partnership must provide each partner with a Schedule K-1 (Form 1065). This schedule details each partner's share of income, gains, losses, deductions, and credits, which the partner then uses to complete their individual or entity tax return. Partners are considered self-employed, rather than employees of the partnership. Consequently, they may be responsible for paying self-employment taxes (Social Security and Medicare) on their share of the income, which is calculated on Schedule SE (Form 1040).

While partnerships are exempt from federal income tax, they are still responsible for other taxes, such as:

1. Employment Taxes: Withholding and paying payroll taxes (FICA and FUTA) for any actual employees (not the partners themselves).
2. Excise Taxes: Taxes on specific goods, services, or activities.
3. Withholding on Foreign Partners: The partnership may be required to withhold and pay tax on income effectively connected with a U.S. trade or business that is allocable to foreign partners.

Corporations (including LLCs)

Trusts and Estates

Detailed guidance on filing requirements and taxpayer responsibilities can be found on the official IRS website. You can also use the USPS Location Finder to locate a place to mail documents.

To calculate your taxes, you should estimate 90% of the tax you owe for the current year compared to the tax you paid in the previous year. Focus on the smaller amount. For example, if you paid $500 last year and estimate your current tax to be $1,000, then 90% of the current estimate would be $900. The smaller amount is $500.

Please note that not all income is subject to estimated tax. For instance, if you work as an independent contractor or freelancer, you may not be obliged to pay estimated taxes on that income. Additionally, dividends, interest, rents, taxable unemployment compensation, retirement benefits, and certain other income sources may also be exempted from estimated tax payments.

To avoid penalties, ensure that you pay your quarterly taxes on time.

Interest Income Overview

Taxable Interest

Taxpayers are generally required to report taxable interest income, which they would typically receive on Form 1099-INT or Schedule K-1 from partnerships and S corporations. Taxable interest can come from various sources, including:

- Bank, savings and loan, or credit union accounts
- Money market funds
- Certificates of deposit
- U.S. treasury bills, notes, and bonds exempt from all state and local income taxes.
- Loans made to others
- Gifts exceeding $10 for opening financial accounts (or $20 if the account balance is over $5,000)
- Interest received on tax refunds
- U.S. Savings Bond Interest

For U.S. Savings Bonds:

- **Series H and HH:** Report semi-annual interest payments in the year they are received.
- **Series I, E, and EE:** Interest is accumulated until maturity. Taxpayers using the cash method of accounting may opt to defer reporting interest until maturity, while those on an accrual basis must report annual accrued interest.

Tip:

Interest from Series I or EE bonds may be tax-exempt if the funds are used for qualified educational expenses within the same year. This exclusion is part of the Education Savings Bond Program and is not applicable for those filing as married filing separately. To claim this exclusion, taxpayers should use Form 8815 and attach it to their Form 1040.

Original Issue Discount (OID)

Original issue discount (OID) represents a form of interest that taxpayers must include as income over the term of a debt instrument, even if no payments are received from the issuer. A debt instrument typically features OID when issued for a price less than its stated redemption price at maturity. The OID is calculated as the difference between the stated redemption price and the issue price. The IRS assumes that all debt instruments that don't pay interest before maturity are issued at a discount. An example of this type is zero-coupon bonds.

The accrual rules for OID generally exclude short-term obligations, which have a fixed maturity date of one year or less from the issue date. If the discount is less than one-fourth of 1% (.0025) of the stated redemption price amortized over the full years from original issue to maturity, it can be treated as zero. This minor discount is referred to as "de minimis" OID.

Dividends and Other Corporate Distributions

Ordinary Dividends

Ordinary dividends are the most common type of distribution from a corporation or mutual fund and are paid out of earnings and profits. These dividends are classified as ordinary income. Generally, taxpayers can assume that any dividends received from common or preferred stock are ordinary dividends unless explicitly stated otherwise by the corporation or mutual fund.

Qualified Dividends

Qualified dividends fall under the category of ordinary dividends but are eligible for a more favorable tax rate compared to other categories of ordinary income. They are subject to the same maximum tax rates (0%, 15%, or 20%) that apply to net capital gains, depending on the taxpayer's taxable income and filing status.

For dividends to qualify for this lower tax rate, the following criteria must be met:

- The dividends must be paid by a U.S. corporation or a qualified foreign corporation.
- They cannot be classified as non-qualified dividends as outlined in Publication 550.

- The taxpayer must hold the stock for over 60 days during the 121-day period that begins 60 days prior to the ex-dividend date. It's important to include the day the stock is sold in the count, but not the day it was acquired. The ex-dividend date is the first day after the declaration of a dividend when the buyer of the stock is no longer entitled to receive the upcoming dividend payment; instead, the seller will receive it.

Income Excluded from Gross Income

Unless excluded by a specific Code provision, all transactions that represent accretions of wealth to the taxpayer are taxable. The Code provides specific exclusions for the following items.

Certain Death Benefits

Gross income generally does not include amounts received (whether in a single sum or otherwise) under a life insurance contract, if such amounts are paid by reason of the death of the insured. This rule does not apply if the taxpayer has received the life insurance policy in a transfer for value (as when the original policy owner transfers the policy to someone else in a business transaction).

Gifts and Inheritances

Gross income does not include the value of property acquired by gift, bequest, devise, or inheritance. Many taxpayers are confused on this point because of the "gift tax" that applies to the maker of the gift.

Interest on State and Local Bonds

Gross income generally does not include interest on any obligation of a State or political subdivision thereof. This exclusion does not apply to any private activity bond that is not a qualified bond, arbitrage bond, or non-registered bond.

Compensation for Injuries or Sickness:

Tax Implications

According to Code section 104(a)(2), gross income excludes damages for personal injuries or physical sickness, but not punitive damages. These damages can come from legal suits or settlements and may be paid in lump sums or installments.

A key case is Nichelle Perez, a California woman who donated eggs and underwent painful medical procedures. She attempted to exclude her payments from taxable income, claiming they were for pain and suffering. However, the court ruled against her, emphasizing that the payments were taxable because they were made under an advance waiver, not as a settlement post-injury.

The court noted that although Perez experienced pain, her voluntary consent to the procedures meant the payments were for services rendered, not as damages for injury. Furthermore, allowing her claim could set a precedent complicating tax classifications for other professions with inherent risks, like professional athletes. Ultimately, the payments were deemed taxable income.

Amounts Received Under Accident and Health Plans

Amounts received by employees through accident or health insurance for personal injuries or sickness are generally excluded from gross income. This applies to amounts that reimburse the taxpayer for medical expenses incurred for themselves, their spouse, dependents, and any child who has not yet reached the age of 27 by the end of the taxable year.

Contributions by Employer to Accident and Health Plans

Typically, gross income for an employee does not include coverage provided by an employer under an accident or health plan. Contributions made by an employer to an Archer Medical Savings Account (MSA) for an employee are considered employer-provided coverage for medical expenses. Similarly, amounts contributed to a health savings account by the employer fall under this category. However, if the coverage includes qualified long-term care services provided through flexible spending arrangements or similar plans, that portion will be included in the employee's gross income.

Rental Value of Parsonages

For ministers of the gospel, their gross income does not account for: (1) the rental value of a home that is provided to them as part of their compensation, and (2) any rental allowance given as part of their compensation, provided that it is used to rent or maintain a home, and does not exceed the fair rental value of the home along with furnishings and utilities. A "minister of the gospel" refers to a clergyman of any faith who is officially ordained, commissioned, or licensed.

Certain Income from Discharge of Indebtedness

While the discharge or cancellation of debt typically results in taxable income, certain exceptions exist where gross income does not include these amounts. These exceptions apply if: **(1)** the discharge occurs in bankruptcy; **(2)** the taxpayer is insolvent at the time of discharge; **(3)** the discharged debt is qualified farm indebtedness; **(4)** for taxpayers other than C corporations, the discharged debt is qualified real property business indebtedness; **(5)** there is a price reduction where the seller lowers the taxpayer's debt while the taxpayer is neither insolvent nor bankrupt; **(6)** the cancellation relates to specific student loan indebtedness; or **(7)** the debt discharged is qualified principal residence indebtedness, provided it is discharged before January 1, 2026.Discharge of certain student loan indebtedness includes:

Excluded from gross income if a creditor cancels debt due to service performance, death, or total disability. Under the Tax

Cuts and Jobs Act of 2017, discharges between December 31, 2017, and January 1, 2026, exclude student loans from gross income. The American Rescue Plan Act of 2021 extends this for discharges after December 31, 2020, until January 1, 2026.

Qualified principal residence indebtedness is related to acquiring or improving a primary home. Debt from refinancing can also qualify, but cash taken out does not. For discharges before January 1, 2021, up to $2 million ($1 million if married filing separately) could be excluded. This exclusion was extended to December 31, 2020, and then to discharges before January 1, 2026, reducing the exclusion to $750,000 ($375,000 for married filing separately) for discharges between 2021 and 2025.

Insolvency exceptions apply only to the extent of insolvency before cancellation. For instance, if liabilities exceed assets by $6,000 and debt of $10,000 is canceled, only $6,000 can be excluded from income, with the remaining $4,000 included.

Recovery of Tax Benefit Items

In general, gross income does not include amounts recovered during the taxable year that were previously deducted in prior years, provided that these deductions did not lower the tax liability. Typically, any recovery of a deducted item must be included in gross income. For instance, if a taxpayer deducted medical expenses in the year 20X0 and later received reimbursement for those expenses from an insurance company in 20X1, they would need to report that reimbursement as part of their gross income for 20X1.

Conversely, if the taxpayer did not itemize their deductions in 20X0, meaning the medical expenses did not lower their tax for that year, the reimbursements received in 20X1 would not need to be included in their income. Similarly, whether a state tax refund is considered taxable income can depend on whether the state tax payment that generated the refund had previously reduced the individual's federal income tax.

Combat Zone Compensation for Members of the Armed Forces

Gross income also excludes certain types of compensation earned by members of the Armed Forces for active service in a combat zone during any month they served. Additionally, this exclusion applies if they were hospitalized due to injuries sustained in the combat zone. However, this exemption does not extend to any hospitalization occurring more than two years after the termination of combat operations in that zone. For commissioned officers, the exclusion is limited to the portion of their compensation that does not exceed the maximum enlisted personnel amount.

Qualified Scholarships

Gross income does not include amounts received as qualified scholarships by individuals pursuing a degree at an accredited educational institution. A "qualified scholarship" refers to funds received as a scholarship or fellowship grant, as long as it is used for qualified tuition and related expenses. These expenses cover tuition, fees necessary for enrollment, and costs for required textbooks, supplies, and equipment for courses at the educational institution. Employees of educational institutions may also benefit from excluded tuition reductions.

There are two notable exceptions to this exclusion. First, any portion of the scholarship that covers room and board is not exempt from taxation. Second, amounts received as payment for teaching, research, or other services required for the scholarship or tuition reduction are also taxable. It is important to note that participation in a school's sports teams does not qualify as a service requirement for the purpose of receiving the scholarship, meaning athletic scholarships are generally excluded from gross income, except for any amount allocated towards room and board.

Meals or Lodging Furnished for the Convenience of the Employer

Gross income does not include the value of meals or lodging provided by an employer for the convenience of the employer. This applies to taxpayers, their spouses, and any dependents. For meals to qualify for this exclusion, they must be provided on the employer's business premises. Similarly, lodging must be accepted on the business premises as a condition of employment to be excluded.

Exclusion of Gain from Sale of Principal Residence

Under Code section 121, taxpayers can exclude a certain amount of gain from the sale or exchange of their principal residence, provided the property has been owned and used as their main home for at least two years within the five-year period prior to the sale. Unmarried taxpayers can exclude up to $250,000, whereas married taxpayers filing jointly may exclude up to $500,000, given they meet specific criteria. It's important to note that this exclusion can only be claimed once every two years.

Amounts Received under Insurance Contracts for Certain Living Expenses

For individuals whose principal residence has been damaged or destroyed by a fire, storm, or other casualty, or who have been denied access to their home due to governmental restrictions, gross income does not account for amounts received from insurance contracts. These amounts are intended to compensate for living expenses incurred due to the loss of use or occupancy of the residence.

Cafeteria Plans

Participants in a cafeteria plan generally do not need to include any amount in their gross income solely because they can choose among the benefits offered by the plan. However, this exclusion does not apply to highly compensated participants if the plan is deemed to discriminate in their favor. Moreover, for key employees, the exclusion will not apply if nontaxable benefits provided to them exceed 25% of the total benefits offered to all employees under the plan.

Educational Assistance Program

Employers have the opportunity to exclude a maximum of $5,250 in educational assistance provided to employees through a formal educational assistance program from the employees' taxable wages each year. This exclusion applies specifically to funds allocated for educational purposes that are separate from payments aimed at enhancing an employee's skills in their current job. As such, education that qualifies under this program can be considered a tax-free fringe benefit.

Dependent Care Assistance Programs

Employers offering dependent care assistance under a formal written plan can exclude these payments from an employee's gross income. However, the exclusion amount cannot surpass the employee's earned income, excluding employer-dependent care assistance payments. For married employees, the exclusion is limited to the earned income of the lower-earning spouse. The maximum allowable exclusion is capped at $5,000 per year ($2,500 for those filing separately). Any amounts exceeding this limit must be included in the employee's taxable income for the year in which the dependent care services were utilized.

It's important to note that to qualify for this exclusion, the employee must provide the name, address, and taxpayer identifying number (TIN) of the individual or organization that supplied the dependent care services on their tax return. Employees can request this information from service providers using Form W-10. If the employee makes a good-faith effort to obtain this information but is unable to, they may not be penalized.

Certain Foster Care Payments

Foster care providers can exclude amounts received as qualified foster care payments from their gross income for the tax year.

Certain Fringe Benefits

According to Code section 132, employers can provide specific tax-free fringe benefits to employees. These include no additional cost services, qualified employee discounts, working condition fringe benefits, de minimis fringe benefits, qualified transportation fringe benefits, and employer-provided retirement advice.

It's important to note that the Tax Cuts and Jobs Act (TCJA) repealed the exclusion for qualified moving expense reimbursements, making them taxable for most employees for taxable years beginning after December 31, 2017, and before January 1, 2026. However, members of the Armed Forces remain exempt from this change.

Certain Military Benefits

Members and former members of the uniformed services of the United States, as well as their dependents, can exclude allowances or in-kind benefits from gross income, with the exception of personal vehicle usage.

Income from United States Savings Bonds Used for Higher Education Tuition and Fees

Under the Education Savings Bond Program, taxpayers can exclude some or all of the interest earned on the redemption of qualified U.S. savings bonds if they apply that interest toward qualified higher education expenses in the same tax year. To qualify for this exclusion, married taxpayers are required to file their tax returns jointly.

Qualified U.S. Savings Bonds:

A qualified U.S. savings bond is defined as a Series EE bond issued after 1989 or a Series I bond. To qualify, the bond must be in the sole name of the taxpayer or jointly held with a spouse. Additionally, the taxpayer must be at least 24 years old by the bond's issue date. It's important to note that the issue date of a bond can be earlier than the purchase date, as it is assigned to the first day of the month in which the bond is purchased.

Qualified Expenses:

Qualified higher educational expenses encompass tuition and fees that are necessary for the taxpayer and any dependents (for whom an exemption is claimed) to attend an eligible educational institution. This category of expenses also includes contributions made to qualified tuition programs or Coverdell education savings accounts. However, it's essential to understand that qualified expenses do not cover costs related to books, room and board, or any courses centered on sports, games, or hobbies unless these are integral to a degree or certificate program.

Eligible Educational Institutions:

Eligible educational institutions consist of most public, private, and nonprofit universities, colleges, and vocational schools that are accredited and participate in federal student aid programs administered by the Department of Education.

Excludable Amount:

Taxpayers may exclude the interest on qualified U.S. savings bonds if the total proceeds (comprised of both interest and principal) from the bonds redeemed during the year do not exceed the adjusted qualified higher education expenses for that year. If the proceeds exceed the expenses, only a portion of the interest may be excluded. To calculate the amount that can be excluded, divide the qualified expenses by the total bond proceeds, then multiply that percentage by the bond interest. Any remaining interest must be included in taxable income.

Modified Adjusted Gross Income Limit:

The income exclusion for interest is subject to phase-out at certain levels of modified adjusted gross income (MAGI). For the tax year 2025, the exclusion begins to phase out for MAGI exceeding $149,250 for joint returns and $99,500 for all other filing statuses. The exclusion is completely phased out for MAGI of $179,250 or more for joint returns and $114,500 or more for other returns.

Energy Conservation Subsidies Provided by Public Utilities:
The value of subsidies provided by public utilities to customers for the purchase or installation of energy conservation measures is excluded from gross income.

Adoption Assistance Programs:
Employees can exclude from their gross income qualified adoption expenses paid or reimbursed by an employer under an adoption assistance program, up to a specified limit per eligible child. For the year 2025, the exclusion for each eligible child is $17,280, even if there are no qualified adoption expenses. For adoptions of children without special needs, the maximum exclusion is either the actual qualified expenses incurred or $17,280, whichever is less.

The amount of adoption assistance excludable from an employee's gross income is also subject to phase-out based on the taxpayer's MAGI. For 2025, the phase-out begins for MAGI above $259,190 and is fully phased out at MAGI of $299,190 or higher.

Tax benefits for adoption include a tax credit for qualified adoption expenses incurred when adopting an eligible child, as well as an exclusion from income for employer-provided adoption assistance. Notably, the tax credit is nonrefundable, which limits it to the taxpayer's tax liability for the year, though any excess credit may be carried forward for up to five years. To prevent double benefits, no adoption credit is available for expenses that have been deducted from taxable income or for which the taxpayer has received funding from federal, state, or local programs.

Disaster relief payments

Disaster relief payments received by individuals are excluded from gross income. This applies to any amounts designated as qualified disaster relief payments that have been officially declared by either the federal government or a state government.

The Challenging Situation 1040

1) Jane's husband moved out of their home in February of the tax year and has not returned. Jane provides all the costs of keeping up the home for herself and her two dependent children. Jane refuses to file a joint return with her husband. What filing status should she use? Answer: filing head of household.
2) Becky and Frank were divorced on December 29 of the tax year. They have no children or other dependents and have not remarried. Their filing status should be: Single
   Cindy's husband died on August 19 of the tax year. Cindy has no dependents and has not remarried. She should file as: Married Filing Jointly
3) Gloria's husband, Dante, has neither a green card nor a visa, and he does not have a tax home in another country. He was physically present in the United States for 150 days in the current tax year and both of the two preceding tax years. Is Dante a resident alien under the substantial presence test for the current tax year? Yes
4) William Burke's wife is a Greek citizen. Her sister, Athena, who is also a Greek citizen, lived in the Burkes' home in Greece for the entire tax year. William provided more than 50 percent of Athena's total support. Can William claim his sister-in-law as a dependent? No
5) Todd and Janet have a MAGI below the threshold limit. They are married and file a joint return. Two years ago,

they took out a loan so Todd's mother could earn her RN degree at night school. Todd could not claim her as a dependent on his return. This year, they paid $1,000 in interest on the loan. Does his mother meet the student qualifications? No. Todd's mother was not their dependent at the time they took out the loan.

6) Cassandra's mother obtained a loan for her daughter's qualified educational expenses. Cassandra, who is her mother's dependent, has agreed to pay the interest on the loan. Who can claim the deduction for student loan interest? Cassandra's mother, who is legally liable for the loan. Because Cassandra made interest payments on behalf of her mother, who is legally obligated to pay the loan, then Cassandra's mother is treated as receiving payments from Cassandra and then making the payments, so the mother is allowed to deduct the payments.
7) Gloria's husband, Dante, has neither a green card nor a visa, and he does not have a tax home in another country. He was physically present in the United States for 150 days in the current tax year and both of the two preceding tax years. Is Dante a resident alien under the substantial presence test for the current tax year? Yes
8) William Burke's wife is a Greek citizen. Her sister, Athena, who is also a Greek citizen, lived in the Burkes' home in Greece for the entire tax year. William provided more than 50 percent of Athena's total support. Can William claim his sister-in-law as a dependent? No
9) Taxpayers preparing their Form 1040 may encounter a variety of rare tax issues that involve complex income sources, international considerations, or specific

deductions and credits that necessitate detailed documentation and particular forms.

Reporting Complex Income and Assets

1. **Digital Assets and Cryptocurrency:** Transactions involving digital assets, such as Bitcoin and NFTs, are classified as property for tax purposes. Taxpayers are required to address a specific question regarding digital assets on Form 1040. Gains and losses from the sale or exchange of these assets should be reported on Form 8949 and Schedule D. Furthermore, any income derived from mining, staking, or receiving cryptocurrency as payment for services is reported as ordinary income and may be subject to self-employment tax.
2. **Foreign Accounts and Investments:** U.S. individuals with an interest in or authority over foreign financial accounts that exceed $10,000 at any point during the year must file a Financial Crimes Enforcement Network (FinCEN) Form 114 (FBAR) with the Treasury Department. Additionally, taxpayers with specified foreign financial assets valued above certain limits—over $50,000 for single filers residing in the U.S. and over $200,000 for those living abroad—must include Form 8938 with their Form 1040.
3. **Passive Foreign Investment Companies (PFICs):** Investments in foreign mutual funds or companies that primarily generate passive income often necessitate the

filing of Form 8621. Ignoring this requirement can lead to complex and potentially severe tax implications.

4. **Estate and Trust Income:** Managing income and expenses from various trusts and estates can be intricate. This often requires professional assistance to ensure that the correct forms (either Form 1040 or Form 1041) are used appropriately.

Overlooked Deductions and Credits

---

1. Reinvested Dividends: Although not strictly a deduction, many taxpayers fail to consider reinvested dividends when determining their tax basis in a stock or mutual fund. This oversight can result in an inaccurately larger taxable capital gain or a smaller loss when shares are sold.
2. Jury Pay Paid to Employer: If an employer continues to pay a worker's full salary during jury duty, and the employee must remit jury fees back to the employer, the taxpayer should report these fees as income. However, they can also claim a corresponding deduction for the amount returned to the employer.
3. Amortizable Bond Premiums: Taxpayers may have the opportunity to deduct amortizable bond premiums, which is a less commonly claimed deduction related to investments.

4. Impairment-Related Work Expenses: Individuals with disabilities may qualify to deduct impairment-related work expenses.
5. Moving Expenses for Military: While the deduction for moving expenses has been largely eliminated for most taxpayers, active-duty military personnel with permanent change of station (PCS) orders may still be able to deduct certain unreimbursed moving costs.

   Taxpayers facing any of these complexities are often advised to consult with a qualified tax professional or utilize specialized tax software to navigate the intricate details and avoid potential penalties.

Understanding Student Taxes and Tax Credits

Taxes apply universally, affecting both students and non-students alike. If individuals earn taxable income, they are obligated to file taxes. Taxable income is calculated by subtracting deductions and credits from total earnings. Depending on individual circumstances, this may result in a refundable amount, commonly referred to as a "refund," or a tax liability, known as "Tax Due." It's important to note that there is no special tax treatment specifically for students, despite common misconceptions.

Recent Changes to 529 Plans

Recent federal legislation, including the One Big Beautiful Bill Act (OBBBA) of 2025 and the existing SECURE 2.0 Act, has significantly transformed the applicability of 529 plans. These changes expand their use beyond traditional four-year college degrees to encompass a variety of educational expenses ranging from K-12 education to vocational training and even retirement savings rollovers.

Key Changes to 529 Plans:

---

1. Expanded K-12 Education Uses

The rules surrounding K-12 expenses have been broadened, enhancing flexibility for families.

A. Increased Withdrawal Limit: Starting January 1, 2026, families can withdraw up to $20,000 per student annually for K-12 expenses, doubling the previous limit of $10,000.

B. Broader Eligible Expenses: As of July 5, 2025, funds can now cover a wider array of K-12 costs, including:

- Curriculum materials, books, and online learning tools
- Tutoring services provided by qualified, non-family professionals
- Fees for standardized tests (e.g., SAT, ACT, AP exams)

- Dual-enrollment college courses taken during high school
- Educational therapies and support for students with disabilities

2. Postsecondary Credentialing and Vocational Training:

529 plans can now support non-traditional education paths, making them a valuable resource for career advancement.

- **Eligible Programs:** Funds may cover expenses for programs that lead to recognized postsecondary credentials, professional licenses, or certifications, such as those in welding, plumbing, cosmetology, or CPA exams.
- **Covered Costs:** Eligible expenses include tuition, fees, books, supplies, equipment, and testing or continuing education fees for approved programs.

3. Rollovers to Roth IRAs

One of the major innovations brought about by the SECURE 2.0 Act is the ability to transfer unused funds from 529 accounts into a Roth IRA. This change addresses concerns regarding overfunding of 529 accounts.

- Lifetime Limit: A total of up to $35,000 can be rolled over during the beneficiary's lifetime.

These updates reflect a significant shift aimed at making educational funding more versatile and accessible for families navigating the evolving landscape of education.

Important Updates on 529 Accounts:

Recent changes to 529 plans have introduced new conditions and opportunities for account holders. Here are the key points:

1. **Eligibility for Rollovers:** To qualify for rollovers, the 529 account must be open for a minimum of 15 years. Additionally, contributions and their earnings made within the last five years are not eligible for rollover.
2. **Annual Limits :** Rollovers from 529 plans to Roth IRAs will be subject to the annual contribution limits set for Roth IRAs. It is also essential that the beneficiary has earned income that meets or exceeds the rollover amount in the corresponding tax year.
3. **ABLE Account Rollovers:** A significant change allows for tax-free rollovers from 529 accounts to ABLE accounts (for individuals with disabilities). This provision has now been made permanent.
4. **Financial Aid Considerations:** Starting with the 2024–2025 academic year, distributions from 529 plans owned by grandparents will no longer be classified as untaxed student income for federal financial aid calculations.
5. **State Compliance:** While these updates are federal changes, individual states will determine whether to align their tax laws accordingly. This means some states might not extend state-level tax benefits for the newly eligible expenses.

These updates enhance the flexibility of 529 plans, presenting new opportunities for families to support a range of educational goals and long-term financial strategies. It is advisable for families to consult with a tax or financial professional to navigate these changes effectively. For further detailed information, the IRS offers comprehensive Q&A resources on 529 plans.

Scholarship Overview

Scholarships often serve as a financial aid resource for students, but it's important to understand their tax implications. Generally, scholarships are tax-free when used for qualified expenses, which include tuition, mandatory fees, books, and other necessary supplies. However, amounts allocated for non-qualified expenses become subject to income tax. These non-qualified expenses might include room and board, travel, and certain required services (like teaching or research), which are reported as taxable income on Form 1040. In instances where the scholarship is a stipend for services, a Form 1099-MISC may be issued.

Tax-Free Scholarship Portion Qualified Expenses

1. **Tuition & Fees:** These are essential expenses related to enrollment or attendance at the institution.
2. **Books, Supplies, Equipment:** These items must be required for your courses to qualify.

Taxable Scholarship Portion Non-Qualified Expenses

1. **Room & Board:** These are living expenses that do not qualify as tax-free.
2. **Travel:** Personal travel costs are also not tax-exempt.
3. **Optional Equipment:** Items that are not required for coursework, such as personal computers, fall under taxable expenses.
4. **Services:** Payments for teaching, research, or other required work usually count as taxable income, unless certain exceptions apply (for example, in specific health programs).

Key Considerations

- Stipends: Be aware that if a scholarship functions as payment for services (like a teaching assistantship), it is generally treated as taxable income.
- Excess Funds: Any amount received that exceeds the required funds for qualified expenses—for instance, a refund—will also be considered taxable income.
- Reporting Requirements: Typically, you will receive a Form 1098-T from your educational institution detailing your payments. Taxable amounts are then reported on your Form 1040, often listed on Line 7 as "Other Income," according to guidelines from H&R Block.

- Tax Credits Impact: Utilizing scholarship funds for non-qualified expenses can negatively affect your eligibility for education tax credits, including the American Opportunity Tax Credit (AOTC).

Understanding these distinctions can help ensure you comply with tax regulations while maximizing your educational funding.

Student Tax Credits Overview

There are two key federal education tax credits designed to help alleviate the financial burden of higher education: the American Opportunity Tax Credit (AOTC) and the Lifetime Learning Credit (LLC). To claim these credits, taxpayers must file Form 8863 with their tax return.

American Opportunity Tax Credit (AOTC)

The AOTC is particularly valuable for undergraduate students, especially those within their first four years of post-secondary education.

- **Maximum Credit:** Eligible students can receive up to $2,500 per year.
- **Refundability:** This credit is partially refundable; up to 40% or up to $1,000 can be received as a refund even if no taxes are owed.

Eligibility Criteria:

- The student must be working towards a degree or recognized education credential.
- Enrollment must be at least half-time for at least one academic term.
- The credit is only applicable during the first four years of higher education.
- Qualified Expenses: These include tuition, required fees for enrollment, and necessary course materials, which encompass books and supplies.

Lifetime Learning Credit (LLC)

The LLC has a broader application, making it available for various educational endeavors. This includes both undergraduate and graduate studies, as well as courses aimed at enhancing job-related skills.

Maximum Credit: This credit allows for a maximum of up to $2,000 per tax return, rather than per student.

Refundability: The LLC is non-refundable, which means it can reduce your tax liability to zero, but any excess amount will not result in a cash refund.

Eligibility Criteria:

- Available for any year of post-secondary education, whether undergraduate or graduate.
- There's no requirement to be pursuing a degree; courses aimed at improving job skills qualify as well.
- No minimum enrollment is necessary; even a single course can be eligible.
- Qualified Expenses: Generally include tuition and necessary fees for enrollment. Books are included only if they are purchased directly from the institution as a requirement for the course.

Key Considerations

- No Double Dipping: Taxpayers cannot claim both the AOTC and LLC for the same student in the same tax year.
- Income Limits: Both credits are subject to Modified Adjusted Gross Income (MAGI) thresholds, which can limit the amount that can be claimed.
- Form 1098-T: Typically, a taxpayer must receive Form 1098-T, Tuition Statement, from an eligible educational institution to claim either credit.

By understanding these credits, students and families can potentially lessen their education costs and make informed financial decisions regarding their higher education investments.

Student Loan Deduction

The student loan interest deduction allows eligible taxpayers to subtract up to $2,500 (or the actual interest paid, if less) from their taxable income. It is an "above-the-line" adjustment, so you can claim it regardless of whether you itemize.

Eligibility Requirements:

- To qualify, you must meet the following criteria:
- You paid interest on a qualified student loan during the tax year.
- You are legally obligated to pay the interest.
- Your filing status is not "Married Filing Separately."

- You or your spouse cannot be claimed as a dependent on someone else's tax return.
- The loan was for you, your spouse, or a dependent when taken out.
- The loan was used for qualified education expenses.
- The education was for a period during which you were enrolled at least half-time.

Key Details for Tax Year 2025:

The deduction remains up to $2,500, but income phase-out ranges have been adjusted:

- Single/Head of Household: MAGI $85,000 - $100,000 (eliminated at $100,000)
- Married Filing Jointly: MAGI $170,000 - $200,000 (eliminated at $200,000)

Other Changes:

- Maximum Deduction: The limit remains $2,500 or actual interest paid.
- Forgiven Debt: Starting in 2026, most forgiven student loan debt will be taxable.
- Employer Assistance: Employers can make tax-free student loan payments up to $5,250, which is now permanent and indexed for inflation.
- Is it a myth or is it a fact? Let's unravel the mystery of the maximum refund!

  In conclusion, the notion that there is a "maximum refund" that everyone can or should receive is a myth. A tax refund is essentially the return of the money you overpaid to the government throughout the year; it is not "free money" or some kind of government bonus or public assistance program.

Key Facts About Tax Refunds

Refunds are based on overpayment: You receive a refund when your tax withholdings or estimated payments surpass your actual tax liability for the year.

There is no set maximum limit:
The size of your refund is determined entirely by your specific income, deductions, and credits.

A large refund means an interest-free loan to the government: If you find yourself receiving a sizable refund, it signifies that you could have enjoyed more money in your paycheck over the course of the year.

The goal is a zero balance: The most tax-efficient outcome is to aim for a tax liability close to zero when you file, meaning you neither have a large amount owed nor receive a substantial refund.

Maximizing Your Take-Home Pay and Minimizing Your Refund

To ensure you are withholding the appropriate amount and avoiding overpayment throughout the year, adjust your W-4 form with your employer accordingly. Utilize the IRS Tax Withholding Estimator tool to pinpoint the right amount to have withheld.

The "Maximum Refund Guarantee" in Tax Software

Tax preparation services such as TurboTax, HR Block and Tax Act promote the term "maximum refund guarantee" to assure customers that their software will identify every eligible deduction and credit based on the information provided, thus calculating the largest possible refund for that individual's unique tax situation. This guarantee does not imply they can secure the largest refund for all taxpayers, but rather the most accurate and comprehensive one tailored to your data.

References

1. IRS. "Forms & Instructions | Internal Revenue Service." *Irs.gov*, 2018, www.irs.gov/forms-instructions.
2. "U.S. Code: Title 26. INTERNAL REVENUE CODE." *LII / Legal Information Institute*, 2011, www.law.cornell.edu/uscode/text/26.
3. "Tax Tips - Articles, Videos, How-Tos, & Tax Guides | TurboTax® Articles." *Intuit.com*, 2024, turbotax.intuit.com/tax-tools/tax-articles-and-tips/.
4. "Homepage." *H&R Block*, 12 Aug. 2024, www.hrblock.com/tax-center/.
5. Segal, Troy. "Why a Tax Credit Is Better than a Tax Deduction." *Investopedia*, 27 Jan. 2022, www.investopedia.com/terms/t/taxcredit.asp.

www.ingramcontent.com/pod-product-compliance
Lightning Source LLC
LaVergne TN
LVHW050912210926
848482LV00012B/414